AI MASTERY FOR BEGINNERS

Simple Strategies and Exercises to Boost Productivity, Spark Creativity, and Advance Your Career

MAURA VELLA

While every effort has been made to ensure the information in this book is accurate and helpful, it's not guaranteed to apply to every situation. The advice and strategies shared here may not be a perfect fit for your unique needs. If you're unsure, it's always a good idea to consult a professional.

The author is not responsible for any losses, damages, or outcomes that may result from using the content in this book. You are responsible for your own decisions, actions, and results.

Disclaimer:

This book is for informational and educational purposes only. It's not a substitute for professional advice, whether legal, financial, medical, or otherwise. Always consult an expert before making big decisions based on what you've read here.

First Edition 2025

CONTENTS

INTRODUCTION

Have you ever wished you could wave a magic wand and create more free time in your day without sacrificing what needs to be done? Perhaps you dream of learning a new skill or taking on a project that once felt out of reach but just haven't found the time yet. Maybe you'd like to streamline your work processes or jumpstart career goals by learning faster and working smarter.

AI makes *all* of these possibilities accessible and attainable—with zero prior experience required.

This book is for anyone wanting to harness AI's potential—whether it be for professional advancement, creative breakthroughs, or a smoother, more balanced day-to-day life.

AI for Beginners, Without the Overwhelm

AI Mastery for Beginners: Simple Strategies and Exercises to Boost Productivity, Spark Creativity, and Advance Your Career guides you through the essentials of integrating AI into your life without the stress. And the best part? If you already know how to work a smartphone, you're more than ready to start. I built this book around practical, accessible tools designed to help you do more in less time, unlock your creative genius, and implement meaningful changes in your routines.

Each chapter explores various AI tools for different areas of life and work, offering hands-on exercises that are easy to follow and designed specifically for beginners. You will learn how to utilize AI to simplify daily tasks, boost productivity, enhance creativity, get ahead in your career, and even support a healthy work-life balance. You'll find that every exercise is approachable and actionable, fostering an AI experience that is both intuitive and rewarding.

Learning at Your Own Pace

This book is designed to meet you where you are. Feel free to explore its contents in a way that aligns with your specific needs, schedule, and interests. You can focus on the sections most relevant to your goals or reference particular parts as needed to enhance your learning experience.

Your hands-on exercises include a complexity scale ranging from 1 (easiest) to 5 (most challenging) to make this journey more manageable. While most exercises take less than 30 minutes to complete, some may require additional time and focus. If you're just starting, consider warming up with a more straightforward exercise before tackling more advanced sections.

Whether you prefer to skip around, dive into specific topics, or work through the book chapter by chapter, this guide is yours to use however it best supports your discovery of AI.

Your AI Toolbox

AI Mastery for Beginners introduces you to over 80 practical AI resources, carefully selected for their accessibility and usefulness. These tools are more than abstract ideas—they're actionable solutions you can start using right away, many of which are free!

That said, technology–especially AI–evolves quickly. While every effort has been made to present up-to-date and reliable tools, some features or platforms mentioned may change over time. Embrace this as part of the journey: exploring new updates and advancements will only deepen your understanding of AI's potential.

You don't need to feel compelled to explore every option listed; they're simply opportunities for you to consider. If something resonates with your needs, give it a try. If not, feel free to move on. *(Quick note: While I recommend these resources based on their value, I am not affiliated with or sponsored by any of the companies mentioned.)*

For easy access, AI resources in **bold** are referenced throughout the book and listed in the glossary at the end. The glossary also includes definitions for unfamiliar terms (also in **bold**), ensuring you feel confident and informed throughout your learning adventure.

Here's an overview of what lies ahead:

- **Chapter 1:** Understand the fundamentals of AI, what it is, and why it matters.
- **Chapter 2:** Discover AI tools that simplify daily routines and save you time.
- **Chapter 3:** Unleash your creativity with generative AI for brainstorming, art, and music.
- **Chapter 4:** See how AI can accelerate career growth and business success.
- **Chapter 5:** Explore AI's impact on your personal life, including fitness, hobbies, and household tasks.
- **Chapter 6:** Learn about ethical considerations, current AI trends, and advancements in the AI sector.
- **Chapter 7:** Experiment with 350 practical ChatGPT prewritten prompts and meta-prompts to increase your productivity, efficiency, and creative inspiration.

A Note on Maintaining Authenticity and Balance

While AI is fantastic for streamlining many aspects of life, it is essential to balance automation with authenticity. This is particularly important for public-facing usage of AI, such as with social media or any type of human engagement. Each tool should *enhance* what you're already doing, *not replace* the unique human touch you bring to your work and relationships.

Ready to Go?

Once you've completed this book, integrating AI into your daily routine should feel like second nature. You may even find yourself adopting a lifestyle where AI regularly helps you free up time, skyrocket productivity, give you an edge in the workplace, and explore a multitude of creative outlets. Whether you're organizing a busy schedule, managing finances, or exploring new hobbies, AI is here as your ally. Every step you take to learn more leads to meaningful results. So let's dive in, explore, and let AI become the catalyst to a more efficient, balanced, and fulfilling life. Your AI adventure starts here.

1

GETTING STARTED WITH AI

Think about the last time **Google Maps** rerouted you to avoid traffic, or when **Spotify** perfectly curated your favorite playlist. Whether you realized it or not, you were actively engaging with AI. These everyday interactions barely scratch the surface of what AI can do. In this chapter, I will briefly cover how AI can fit effortlessly into your life, and thus enhance your productivity, open new career doors, and give you back precious time to do what you love. As you'll soon find out, embracing the full potential of AI empowers you to achieve more than you ever thought possible.

1.1 WHAT IS AI AND WHY SHOULD YOU CARE?

So, what exactly is AI? Let's break it down. **Artificial Intelligence**, or **AI,** refers to designing machines that can mimic human learning, reasoning, and decision-making processes. Think of AI as a digital brain; just as your own brain processes information and makes decisions, AI takes in data, analyzes it, and makes intelligent predictions or choices. While your brain might need an extra cup of coffee to function at its best, AI never needs a break and works tirelessly around the clock.

Real-World AI Examples

Chances are you use AI way more often than you think. Whenever you have **Siri** remind you about an appointment, ask **Alexa** about the weather, or let **Google Photos** organize your pictures, *you're tapping into AI*. Platforms such as **Netflix** and **Amazon** use AI regularly to recommend content or products, predicting what visitors would like to see based on their past interactions. These systems quietly mold themselves into our daily activities, making life a bit easier and more efficient without us even realizing it.

Why AI Matters

So, why should AI be on your radar right now? For one, it has the potential to significantly elevate your productivity to new levels. Imagine a set of tools that automate routine tasks such as managing emails, organizing schedules, or drafting reports—freeing you up to focus more on the impactful and creative aspects of your work. By taking the burden of mundane activities off your shoulders, AI doesn't just save time; it reduces mental clutter, allowing for sharper focus and greater output.

Here's the most exciting part: AI isn't just enhancing everyday tasks—it's transforming entire industries. From healthcare to finance, sectors worldwide are increasingly powered by AI-driven solutions, giving professionals who can leverage this technology a significant edge. AI has the ability to analyze complex data, support informed business decisions, and predict emerging trends, making it an invaluable tool for those looking to get ahead. Whether you want to stand out in your current role or explore future career opportunities, AI proficiency opens once-unimaginable doors, positioning you as a vital asset in any field.

The benefits of AI aren't limited to the workplace, either. AI can simplify your personal life in a number of ways. For example, **smart home devices** powered by AI adjust thermostats automatically or monitor security systems while you're out of the house. AI-enabled fitness apps track progress and suggest personalized workout plans, helping you stay on top of your health goals. Even your shopping experience becomes more efficient with AI recommending products based on your purchase history. These tools aren't just readily available; they're already being integrated into our daily lives.

Key Takeaways:

- AI automates repetitive tasks, improves decision-making, and boosts productivity, allowing you more time to focus on creative and strategic work.
- You're likely already using AI in everyday apps such as **Google Maps**, **Siri,** and **Netflix**.
- Learning how to leverage AI can give you a competitive edge in your career and enhance your personal life.

1.2 DEMYSTIFYING AI: SIMPLE TERMS, BIG IDEAS

Machine Learning: Technology That Thinks and Adapts

You may have heard the term **machine learning** before, but what does that mean exactly? Machine learning is a field within AI that allows computers to continuously improve their performance by learning from data, much like a child learning to identify animals from pictures. Think of showing a child numerous images of cats and dogs while telling them which is which. Over time, they get better at telling them apart and are able to identify them separately. Similarly, machine learning works by feeding computers tons of data so they can learn to make predictions or decisions. It's a lot like having a digital buddy who gets smarter with the more information they absorb.

Take Netflix, for example. Whenever you watch a movie or series, machine learning analyzes your viewing habits and recommends more content that you might enjoy. AI is constantly *learning* from your preferences to offer better and more relevant suggestions over time.

Now, let's explore the relationship between **AI**, **machine learning**, and **deep learning**. Picture AI as the umbrella term that covers everything related to how machines act intelligently. Under this umbrella, machine learning allows computers to learn from data and make decisions without being explicitly programmed. Deep learning takes this a step further and expands the horizons of AI's capabilities.

Deep Learning: Taking AI One Step Further

Let's go deeper down the AI rabbit hole—literally and figuratively. **Deep learning** is a highly advanced subset of machine learning. Think of deep learning as a massive orchestra playing a symphony. In traditional machine learning, you might hear a solo musician playing a simple melody—it works for straightforward tasks. Deep learning, however, is the full orchestra. Each instrument (neuron in the neural network) contributes a unique part, working in harmony across multiple layers to produce a complex and beautiful symphony of insights. Just as the orchestra layers sounds to create depth and richness, deep learning processes massive amounts of data through layers of networks to reveal intricate patterns and solutions.

You may not realize it, but you interact with deep learning technology daily! **Voice assistants** like Siri or Alexa rely on deep learning to recognize and respond to your voice commands. **Facial recognition technology**, used in various apps or to unlock mobile phones, also uses deep learning to identify and match facial features. These tools require the power of deep learning to detect patterns and make sense of large **datasets**.

You now have a better understanding of how AI, machine learning, and deep learning are all related and how they work together. This foundation will help you confidently explore how AI works behind the scenes in your everyday apps and tools.

Key Takeaways:

- **Machine learning** allows computers to acquire information from data and improve over time, while **deep learning** handles more complex patterns using **neural networks**.
- We interact with AI and deep learning on a daily basis through tools like **voice assistants** and **facial recognition.**
- AI, **machine learning**, and **deep learning** work together to make modern technology more innovative and intelligent.

1.3 THE ROLE OF DATA: WHAT EVERY BEGINNER SHOULD KNOW ABOUT AI

Data is AI's Fuel

At the core of every AI system is data—lots of it. Data is the fuel that powers AI's ability to learn, adapt, and make decisions. Think of data as the raw material AI needs to recognize patterns and generate insights. Just as humans can only make informed decisions based on information available to them, AI relies on data to understand and interact with the world.

For example, when an AI-powered **virtual assistant** like Siri recognizes your voice, there's more than magic at work here. AI has been taught and trained on enormous speech datasets, allowing it to understand different accents, tones, and languages. The more data it processes, the better it gets at understanding what you're saying and providing a helpful response.

Quality Over Quantity

Not all data is created equal, however. AI thrives on *quality* data input — meaning accurate, relevant, and clean data. Just as providing someone with bad information can lead to poor decision-making, flawed data leads to poor outcomes in AI systems. That's why **organizing data**—removing errors and inconsistencies—is crucial. But don't worry; you likely won't have to deal with this technical side of AI. Just remember that behind every intelligent AI system is a carefully prepared data engine.

One of AI's greatest strengths is its ability to quickly process vast amounts of data—far more rapidly than any human could. This allows AI to spot trends, make recommendations, and predict outcomes with impressive speed and accuracy. Whether used in healthcare, where AI scans thousands of medical images to diagnose conditions, or in finance, where stock market trends are analyzed, data is the fuel that drives AI's potential.

In a nutshell, data is the most essential ingredient in AI—without it, AI wouldn't exist. And as more data becomes available, AI's potential will continue to expand. This information will help you better understand how AI-driven tools are leveraged for productivity in the coming chapters.

Key Takeaways:

- **Data** is the core of AI systems, enabling them to learn, adapt, and make decisions.
- AI thrives on high-quality data; bad data leads to bad results.
- AI's ability to quickly process large datasets makes it an incredibly powerful tool across numerous industries.

1.4 DEBUNKING COMMON MISCONCEPTIONS ABOUT AI

AI may seem like a modern breakthrough, but its roots stretch back to the 1950s. Decades ago, researchers introduced foundational concepts like neural networks and machine learning algorithms. Thanks to these milestones, advancements in computing power and access to large datasets have since accelerated AI's development. While AI's capabilities have surged in recent years, its long history reveals that it's more than a fleeting trend— it's a proven field with long-term significance in shaping the future.

A common belief and fear shared by many is that AI will replace jobs, leading to widespread unemployment. Even though AI will undoubtedly change the nature of work, embracing it as a tool that enhances human abilities rather than replaces them is a more realistic outlook. We can instead think of AI as an assistant who handles repetitive or routine tasks, allowing us to focus on more complex, creative, and meaningful aspects of our day. For instance, in customer service, AI **chatbots** manage basic inquiries, leaving human agents to handle more nuanced or challenging issues. This collaboration allows workplaces to be more productive and efficient. In fact, the World Economic Forum estimates that AI will create 97 million new jobs in 2025 in areas like AI ethics, data analysis, and system maintenance—surpassing the number of jobs it might replace.

Another misconception is that AI can only be used by tech experts. Although AI was once the domain of specialists, modern AI tools are now easily accessible to anyone. You don't need a background in computer science to use AI effectively. Today's AI platforms, such as **ChatGPT**, allow you to interact with AI through simple text **prompts**—whether you're drafting emails, brainstorming ideas, or managing daily tasks. These tools are intuitive and require zero coding skills. As AI continues to develop, learning resources are becoming increasingly available as well, with beginner-friendly books (like this one!), courses, and community forums that make it easier than ever to get started.

Lastly, it's important to note that AI is not perfect. Despite their advanced **algorithms**, AI systems can and do make mistakes. For example, AI facial recognition systems have misidentified individuals, and healthcare AI tools have made incorrect diagnoses due to limitations in training data. These errors highlight the crucial need for human oversight. While AI is a highly effective tool, it cannot replace human judgment. Regular monitoring and evaluation of AI systems is essential to ensure that AI functions correctly and ethically as it evolves.

Addressing these misconceptions helps clarify that AI is a tool meant to enhance human potential. It's accessible to everyone, yet still requires human oversight, and has been evolving for decades. As AI continues to grow, its impact will be noticeable in all areas of life, providing new opportunities and transforming industries in exciting ways.

Now that you have a better understanding of what AI is—and what it isn't—it's time to make it a practical part of your daily life. The first step is choosing the right tools and creating a productive environment. With the proper setup, AI can help you work smarter, accomplish more, and attain your goals that much faster.

Key Takeaways:

- AI has been evolving for over 70 years and is not just a modern trend but a professional field with long-term impact.
- AI will not replace all jobs and will, in fact, create millions of jobs in the future.
- AI is accessible to everyone, not just tech experts, with user-friendly tools designed for beginners.

1.5 GETTING COMFORTABLE WITH YOUR FIRST AI TOOLS

Finding the right tools is the first step in making AI a practical part of your daily life. But with so many options available, it's easy to feel overwhelmed. This is why it's best to start small and focus on what matters most to you.

For beginners, it's easiest to start with one tool that fits your immediate needs. **ChatGPT** is an excellent option because it's simple, user-friendly, and can handle everyday tasks: writing emails, generating creative ideas, managing to-do lists, etc. It doesn't require any coding knowledge either, making it an ideal starting point for those new to AI. I will refer to ChatGPT often throughout this book due to its versatility and ease of use.

But what if your goals are more specific? Maybe you're hoping to automate a few routine tasks or need help with a creative project. Here's a suggestion: before exploring multiple tools, consider how you want AI to help you the most. Focus on your big picture goal, then choose a tool that aligns with it. How do you find an AI tool? **Google** it!

Welcome to our first hands-on exercise, where you'll learn how to discover new and trending AI tools.

Hands-On Exercise: Finding a New AI Tool

Complexity Rating: 1/5

Estimated Time: 15-20 minutes

This exercise will guide you through finding and experimenting with an AI tool that matches your needs. Whether you're looking to automate routine tasks, spark creativity, or improve productivity, this step-by-step approach will help you get started.

1. **Define Your Goal:** Decide what you want AI to help you with. Writing down your specific goals will help you find a tool that aligns perfectly with your needs.
2. **Search for the Right Tool:** Open **Google** and type in a search query based on your goal. For example, if you're looking to create blog post outlines, try searching for *"easy AI tool for creating blog outlines"* or *"AI tool for beginners content creation."* Google will then display a range of relevant options.
3. **Review and Select:** Browse through the search results while focusing on descriptions and user reviews. Look for tools that are beginner-friendly and specifically address your needs. Choose one that looks promising and offers a free trial or basic version.
4. **Watch a Quick Tutorial:** Head over to **YouTube** and search for a helpful tutorial video on the tool you've chosen. For example, if you selected **Copy.ai**, search *"Copy.ai tutorial for beginners."* A short video can help you understand the basics before diving in further.
5. **Sign Up and Explore:** Sign up for a free trial or basic version of the tool. Don't feel pressured to explore all of its features—focus on the basics that relate to your goal.
6. **Test with a Simple Task:** Try out a small, manageable task to get a feel for the tool. If you're using Copy.ai, generate a blog post introduction on a topic of your choice, such as *"The Benefits of AI in Daily Life."* Simply enter the topic into the tool, select a relevant tone, and review the output to see how it

crafts engaging content. Adjust the input or tone to experiment with different styles.

7. **Reflect on Your Experience:** After using the tool, take a moment to reflect. Was it easy to use? Does it help solve your problem? If it seems useful, consider keeping it in your routine. If it doesn't quite meet your needs, continue searching for a different tool.
8. **Gradually Explore More:** Once you're comfortable with the tool's basics, start exploring its additional features. As you become more familiar with it, you'll find other ways to make it even more useful.

Pro Tips:

- **Leverage Free Resources:** Explore **YouTube**, **Reddit**, and online forums for feedback and how-to guides on specific tools.
- **Take Your Time:** Start with small tasks, gain confidence, and gradually explore more as needed.

Every successful interaction with AI gradually builds your momentum and comfort, preparing you for more advanced usage over time. There's no need to figure everything out all at once—start by testing one or two tools that meet your immediate needs. Most AI platforms offer free or trial versions, allowing you to explore without commitment. YouTube and Reddit are also excellent for user feedback and tutorials, providing valuable insights along the way.

The aim is to keep your AI journey enjoyable and straightforward. Stick with tools that feel natural to you, and take your time getting to know them. There's no rush—start small, build your confidence, and let each win guide your next step. As you become more comfortable, you can gradually explore additional tools that also align with your goals.

Key Takeaways:

- Start by using one tool that suits your needs, and explore free versions before committing.
- Focus on your goals to find the right AI tool, and test out tools gradually to build confidence.
- Use additional resources like tutorials and community forums to learn more and optimize your use of AI.

1.6 CHATGPT 101: YOUR PERSONAL AI ASSISTANT

Now that you've started exploring AI tools let's look at one of the most versatile options available: **ChatGPT**. Have you ever wondered what it would be like to have a personal assistant who's available 24 hours a day, seven days a week, 365 days per year, who never tires, and can help you tackle a wide variety of tasks? Whether you need to draft a flawless email, a list of creative ideas for a project, or a reorganization of your daily to-do list, ChatGPT is a powerful tool and dependable partner for both creative and practical challenges.

What is ChatGPT?

ChatGPT, developed by **OpenAI**, is a conversational AI that works by generating human-like responses based on the **prompts** you provide. It's like having a brilliant, always-available assistant who can help with tasks ranging from content creation and brainstorming to technical solutions like coding and data analysis.

At its core, ChatGPT is intuitive and accessible to anyone—yes, even if you don't have a technical background. Its effectiveness depends heavily on how you frame your prompts, which act like a starting point for its answers. Think of prompts like planting a seed: the clearer and more specific your prompt, the better the response will *"grow."* Over time, refining your prompts allows ChatGPT to deliver increasingly accurate, insightful, and tailored results.

Best Practices for Writing Effective ChatGPT Prompts

To get the most out of ChatGPT, keep in mind these best practices when crafting your prompts:

- **Be Specific:** The more details you include, the better the response will be. Instead of *"Write an email,"* try *"Write an email to my boss asking for time off next week for a family event."*
- **Use Role-Based Prompts:** Asking ChatGPT to *"act as"* an expert in a specific field can improve responses. For example, *"Act as a career coach and help me write a resume objective for a marketing position."*
- **Add Constraints or Requirements:** Set parameters such as time, length, or format to get tailored responses. For instance, *"Suggest a healthy dinner recipe that takes under 20 minutes to cook."*
- **Provide Context:** Share background information to guide ChatGPT's responses. For example, *"Draft a casual email to my colleague thanking them for their help with last week's report."*
- **Stick to one question or task at a time**: Avoid asking multiple questions in a single prompt. Instead of *"What are some marketing tips, and how do I boost my social media?"* break it into two separate requests.

Things to Keep in Mind

While ChatGPT is a powerful assistant, it's not perfect. Here are some considerations to ensure you use it effectively:

- **Refining is Key:** Don't expect perfect results the first time around. If the first response isn't quite right, clarify or adjust your prompt with more details for better outcomes.
- **Occasional Inaccuracies in Information:** ChatGPT might provide incorrect or outdated information. Always verify critical facts and cross-check with trusted sources.
- **No Real-Time Awareness:** ChatGPT doesn't have access to live data or recent events and may not provide up-to-date information.

- **Simulated Expertise Only:** While ChatGPT can simulate expertise, it is not a substitute for advice from certified professionals like doctors, lawyers, or financial advisors.
- **Bias in Responses:** Because ChatGPT is trained on varied data, responses may reflect biases. (We'll explore this more in the Ethics chapter.)
- **Use It as a Tool, Not a Replacement:** ChatGPT enhances your ideas and workflow but should not replace human creativity, decision-making, or judgment.

By understanding these limitations, you'll be able to navigate ChatGPT's capabilities effectively and maximize its value.

What's the Difference: Free vs. Paid Versions

Setting up ChatGPT is easy. You'll start by visiting **OpenAI**, where you can choose between a basic free version or a paid version with more advanced features:

- **Free Version:** This gives you access to essential ChatGPT functions; these are great for writing, brainstorming, or managing daily activities. However, you might encounter slower responses or temporary access limitations during peak usage.
- **Paid Version:** For those who need more advanced features, faster response times, or priority access during busy periods, the paid version offers an upgraded experience. By subscribing to the paid plan, you'll have more robust access to additional capabilities and improvements as the platform evolves.

By understanding these limitations, you'll be able to navigate ChatGPT's capabilities effectively and maximize its value.

Hands-On Exercise: Trying Out ChatGPT

Complexity Rating: 1/5

Estimated Time: 5 minutes

Learn first-hand the power of refining prompts for a more useful response.

1. **Open ChatGPT**: Sign up for a free account.
2. **Start with a Simple Prompt:** Enter the following prompt: *"Can you give me a simple pasta recipe with garlic, tomatoes, and basil?"*
   - Review the response and take note of how well it meets your expectations.
3. **Refine the Prompt:** Now, repeat Step 2 but with some minor adjustments. Try refining your prompt by saying, *"Act as a professional chef and suggest a pasta recipe with garlic, tomatoes, and basil that can be made in under 30 minutes."*
   - Notice how much more detailed and specific the second response is compared to the first.
4. **Brainstorm Further Uses:** Think about other ways you could use ChatGPT, such as creating an outline for a business plan or organizing a week of budget-friendly, healthy dinners for a family of four. Try a few different prompts to get a feel for how ChatGPT can fit into your daily workflow. The more you experiment, the more you'll see how ChatGPT adapts to your needs.

Incorporating ChatGPT into Your Routine

Now that you've seen how easy it is to use ChatGPT, think about how you can incorporate it into your daily routine. Whether you're using it to generate ideas, streamline your to-do list, or tackle professional challenges, ChatGPT can quickly become an essential tool in your productivity toolkit.

With consistent use, you'll develop the confidence to write better prompts, explore new ways to leverage its features and discover just how much time and effort this AI assistant can save.

Key Takeaways:

- **ChatGPT** is a versatile AI that can assist with tasks like drafting emails and generating ideas by responding to clear, specific prompts.
- The free version is adequate for everyday use, while the paid version offers more advanced features.
- Mastering ChatGPT happens by refining your prompts to get the most accurate and beneficial responses.

2

AI TOOLS FOR DAILY PRODUCTIVITY

We've already looked at the basics of AI, but now let's look at how these tools can make a real impact on your daily productivity. Whether you're juggling work tasks, personal errands, or just trying to stay organized, AI can help streamline your routines and keep you on track. In this chapter, we'll explore practical ways to incorporate AI into everyday life—starting with one of the most accessible tools: virtual assistants.

2.1 KICKSTARTING YOUR DAY WITH VIRTUAL ASSISTANTS

Virtual assistants like **Siri**, **Alexa**, and **Google Assistant** are more than just gadgets for setting alarms or checking the weather. When used thoughtfully, they can be powerful partners in managing your schedule, helping with to-do lists, setting reminders, and even automating repetitive tasks—all through simple voice commands. Having your assistant handle these small but essential tasks frees up mental space and precious time to focus on more important matters.

A Real-Life Example: Streamlining Your Morning with Alexa

Imagine starting your day with a programmed routine engineered to keep you informed, organized, and energized. You wake up to a daily weather report, appointment reminders for the day, updates on important news events, and a music playlist to get you moving. With a virtual assistant like Alexa, this productivity boost is just a few voice commands away.

Here's what a simple, AI-enhanced morning routine might look like:

1. **[7:00 a.m.]** Alexa plays your favorite morning playlist to energize you for the day ahead.
2. **[7:05 a.m.]** Alexa shares the weather forecast: *"Good morning! Today's weather is sunny, with a high of 72°F."*
3. **[7:45 a.m.]** Alexa reminds you of the day's schedule: *"You have a meeting at 9:00 a.m. Don't forget to review the project notes."*
4. **[8:00 a.m.]** Alexa provides top news headlines to keep you informed.

With a simple voice command like, *"Alexa, start my morning routine,"* you've automated the delivery of vital information so you can start the day feeling organized and focused.

This customized routine can help you clear your mind, save time, and set a productive tone for the day—all without needing to pick up your phone or check multiple apps.

Getting Started with Your Virtual Assistant

You might already be familiar with a few of the most popular virtual assistants, but here's a quick refresher:

- **Alexa**: Amazon's AI assistant is known for controlling smart home devices, playing music, setting timers, and managing shopping lists.

- **Google Assistant**: Google's AI can help you manage your schedule, control smart devices, check the weather, and answer all sorts of questions quickly.
- **Microsoft Co-Pilot**: An AI assistant in Microsoft 365 apps that streamlines tasks like creating documents, analyzing data, and generating presentations.
- **Siri**: Apple's voice-activated assistant can help with everything from setting reminders and sending messages to controlling smart home devices.

Simply activate your assistant by voice or by pressing a button, and you're ready to go. Each assistant learns your unique preferences over time, making it smarter and more efficient with every interaction.

Hands-On Exercise: Automating Your Morning Routine and Managing Tasks

Complexity Rating: 1/5

Estimated Time: 10-15 minutes

Put your favorite virtual assistant to work by automating simple morning tasks. This exercise will help you set up reminders, manage to-do lists, and streamline your morning updates in just a few easy steps.

1. **Identify Your Morning Priorities:** Think about what tasks or updates would help you start your day smoothly. Examples might include:
    - Check your calendar for appointments or deadlines
    - Getting a quick weather update
    - Starting a to-do list for the day
2. **Ask for Updates with Voice Commands:** Get comfortable with your assistant by asking for useful updates, like weather or traffic, on demand. Try these simple voice commands:
    - *"Siri, what's the weather today?"*

  - *"Alexa, what's the traffic like on my way to work?"*
  - *"Hey Google, tell me the weather and top news."*
3. **Enable Calendar Access:** To have your assistant announce appointments or daily tasks, link your digital calendar:
   - Open your assistant's app (e.g., **Alexa**, **Google Home**, or **Shortcuts**)
   - Navigate to **Settings** or **Calendar Settings**
   - Link your preferred calendar (e.g., **Google Calendar**, **Apple Calendar**, **Outlook**) by following the on-screen prompts
   - Once linked, try asking, *"What's on my calendar today?"*
4. **Manage Your To-Do List:** Let your assistant help you organize and review your tasks for the day:
   - *"Siri, remind me to pick up my prescription from the pharmacy at 3 p.m. today."*
   - *"Alexa, add 'Submit report' and 'Prepare for tomorrow's meeting' to my to-do list."*
   - *"Hey Google, what's on my to-do list today?"*
5. **Explore Routines for More Automation:** Combine multiple tasks into one automated command using your assistant's app:
   - Open the **Alexa app**, **Shortcuts app**, or **Google Home app**
   - Look for **Routines** or **Shortcuts** and follow the steps to create your custom routine
   - Bundle tasks like weather updates, reminders, and news into a single command, triggered by a phrase or time
6. **Set Up a Routine:** Once your routine is created, activate it with a single command:
   - *"Siri, run my morning shortcut."*
   - *"Alexa, start my morning routine."*
   - *"Hey Google, good morning."*

This simple setup will help you start your day with clarity and focus, ensuring nothing important slips through the cracks. As you get comfortable, experiment with adding new tasks or updates to your routine to make mornings even smoother.

Key Takeaways:

- Virtual assistants can streamline mornings by automating tasks like weather updates and reminders.
- Start with simple voice commands and gradually integrate to-do list management and calendar access.
- As you gain confidence, explore advanced features like creating custom routines for added efficiency.

2.2 WRITING EMAILS THAT SHINE WITH CHATGPT

Now that you've learned to leverage AI virtual assistants to stay organized, let's turn to another essential skill—writing unmistakably effective emails. For many, writing emails can feel like a chore. Whether you're drafting a quick message to a colleague or crafting a more formal email to a client, getting the tone, structure, and content right can be time-consuming. Fortunately, AI tools like **ChatGPT** can simplify the process, helping you write emails in less time that also convey your message effectively.

With ChatGPT, you have a powerful writing assistant at your fingertips. It can help you write professional emails, personalize messages, and even generate polite responses to tricky situations. Best of all, ChatGPT can help you draft emails with the right tone—whether it's formal, friendly, or somewhere in between.

Getting Started: Writing Emails Using ChatGPT

ChatGPT for email writing is intuitive and straightforward. Open ChatGPT in your browser or app, and start by typing a prompt such as, *"Draft an email to my boss asking for feedback on my recent project."* ChatGPT will generate an email template for you, which you can tweak as needed. For even better results, provide clear and detailed context so it can deliver responses that fully meet your needs.

For example, a clear and detailed prompt could be: *"Write a polite and professional email to my manager asking for feedback on my recent presentation about our sales strategy. Please include an opening sentence thanking them for their time and a closing line requesting a follow-up meeting."*

Notice how the prompt gives clear instructions on what the email should include, which makes ChatGPT's response more tailored and relevant. The more specific you are with your input, the better the output will be.

Crafting the Right Email Tone

Tone is fundamental when writing emails, and ChatGPT excels at adjusting tone based on your needs. Whether it's a formal email to a client or a friendly message to a colleague, ChatGPT can modify the phrasing to match your requirements. To help guide ChatGPT, you can include tone instructions in your prompt, such as:

- **Professional**: Use this for formal business emails, such as sending an official request or update.
  - *Example: "Write a professional email to inform my team about the upcoming project deadline."*
- **Friendly and Casual**: Best for messages between colleagues or to keep things light and approachable.
  - *Example: "Draft a casual email thanking my colleague for help with the presentation."*
- **Polite But Direct**: Useful for following up on something without sounding pushy.
  - *Example: "Write a polite but direct email asking for feedback on the draft I sent earlier."*
- **Warm and Encouraging**: Perfect for situations where you want to express appreciation or give positive feedback.
  - *Example: "Draft a warm email thanking my team for their hard work on the latest project."*
- **Formal and Diplomatic**: Ideal for delicate situations where you need to be careful with wording, such as addressing a sensitive issue.

  - *Example: "Write a formal and diplomatic email addressing the recent changes in our department structure."*
- **Concise and To The Point**: Great for short, no-frills communication when you just need to get the facts across quickly.
  - *Example: "Write a concise email requesting updated information on the client's preferences."*

Feel free to experiment with these tones or suggest some of your own. Try incorporating them into your ChatGPT prompts to see how the tone of your email shifts; it's a great way to refine your communication for different audiences and contexts!

Hands-On Exercise: Using ChatGPT to Write a Follow-Up Email

Complexity Rating: 1/5

Estimated Time: 5-10 minutes

Let's put **ChatGPT** to the test by having it help you write a follow-up email. This example could typically be tricky to phrase, but ChatGPT can easily handle it:

1. **Open ChatGPT and Start with a General Prompt:** Type the following prompt to get the initial draft of a follow-up email:
   - *"Write a professional follow-up email to a client, thanking them for their time during a meeting and asking if they have any additional questions about the project we discussed."*
2. **Review the First Draft:** Take a moment to evaluate the first response ChatGPT generates. While it may be helpful, remember this is just the starting point.
   - Ask yourself: *Does it capture the tone I want? Is the message clear and direct? Is there any missing information?*
   - If the draft is missing something, move on to Step 3 for refinement.

3. **Refine for Specific Needs and Details:** It's time to personalize the email. For example, if you want to set up a meeting or add more specific details, refine the prompt:
   - *"Please add a sentence to schedule a follow-up meeting next week to review project updates."*
   - If the response feels too formal or casual for your style, adjust the tone by typing a prompt like: *"Make this email sound more casual and friendly."*
   - Alternatively, if your client prefers formal communication, you could say: *"Please make the email more formal and professional."*
4. **Refine for Length and Focus:** Ensure the email isn't too long or overwhelming for the recipient. If needed, refine the draft further by saying: *"Shorten the email and make it more concise while keeping the essential details."* This prompt will help you strike the right balance between clarity and brevity, an essential aspect of follow-up emails.
5. **Include a Call-to-Action (CTA) if Necessary:** A well-written email often ends with a clear call-to-action. If you need ChatGPT to add one, type: *"Include a call-to-action requesting the client's availability for next steps."*
6. **Final Review:** Once ChatGPT has refined the email, review it again to ensure it meets your expectations. At this point, the email should feel tailored, polished, and ready to send.
7. **Send the Email:** Once you're happy with the email, use it to guide your final draft. Customize it with personal details, then send it confidently, knowing ChatGPT helped you craft the perfect message.

This exercise demonstrates how ChatGPT can do more than draft basic emails—it allows you to refine communication, free up time, and produce emails that feel professional, strategic, and aligned with your goals. By following these steps, you'll see how AI enhances your ability to manage communication effortlessly while maintaining a polished and personal touch.

Best Practices for Writing Emails with ChatGPT:

- **Be specific with your prompts**: The more details you give ChatGPT, the better the output will be. For example, if you need a formal email, mention that in the prompt. If you want specific information included, incorporate that as well.
- **Review and tweak**: ChatGPT's first draft may not be perfect. Don't hesitate to make minor edits and ensure the email sounds like you.
- **Use ChatGPT for brainstorming**: Not sure how to begin an email? Ask ChatGPT for a list of subject lines or opening sentences to help you get started. Identify the essential points you want to communicate, then ask ChatGPT to organize and refine them into a clear, well-structured email. This approach ensures your message is organized and conveyed effectively.

Writing emails doesn't have to be a time-consuming or overwhelming task. With the proper prompts and enough practice, ChatGPT can transform email writing from a chore into an efficient, streamlined process. Through refining prompts and leveraging tone adjustments, ChatGPT will become an invaluable asset in your communication toolkit.

Key Takeaways:

- **ChatGPT** can help you write professional, clear, and effective emails with minimal effort.
- Being specific with your prompts improves the quality of the output.
- Don't be afraid to suggest tone adjustments or include additional details based on your needs.

2.3 SIMPLIFYING SCHEDULING AND CALENDAR MANAGEMENT WITH AI

Managing a busy schedule can be challenging, yet staying on top of it all is possible with the right tools. Earlier in the chapter, we introduced basic scheduling functions using virtual assistants. Now, let's explore how specialized AI-powered tools can take calendar management to a new level. These tools go beyond setting simple reminders; they intelligently organize your time, prevent scheduling conflicts, and streamline your daily routines with minimal effort.

How AI Scheduling Tools Improve Productivity and Reduce Stress

AI-driven calendar tools take the hassle out of scheduling by automating time-consuming tasks like finding ideal meeting times, preventing scheduling conflicts, and managing reminders. By handling these logistics, AI scheduling tools allow you to focus on your work without distractions.

For instance, AI tools automatically suggest the best meeting time slots based on everyone's availability, time zones, and work hours, eliminating the back-and-forth of manual coordination. They also integrate seamlessly with your calendar to prevent double-booking, alerting you to potential conflicts and organizing your commitments.

These tools also handle reminders and follow-ups, sending automated alerts for upcoming meetings and deadlines. After a meeting, they can prompt you to add action items or even provide you with a meeting summary, ensuring that important details are captured effortlessly.

If unexpected events arise, AI tools make rescheduling easy by adjusting meeting times and notifying participants on your behalf. This flexibility keeps your calendar accurate and up-to-date, reducing the need for constant manual updates.

With these features, AI scheduling tools provide a smoother, more efficient scheduling experience, helping you stay focused without the stress of managing your calendar.

AI-Powered Tools for Smarter Scheduling and Time Management

AI scheduling tools do more than just create events on a calendar. By learning your habits, preferences, and daily rhythms, AI lets you take control of your time with minimal manual input. Here's an overview of some top tools and their capabilities:

- **Apple Reminders:** A built-in task management app for Apple users that syncs across devices via iCloud. It lets you create reminders, set location-based alerts, and organize tasks into lists for easy management of personal or work tasks.
- **Calendly**: A scheduling tool that syncs with your calendar to simplify booking. Share your link, and others can schedule meetings based on your availability, eliminating the back-and-forth emails. This resource is ideal for teams and businesses managing many meetings.
- **Google Tasks**: A simple task management tool that integrates with Google Calendar and Gmail. Create, prioritize, and check off to-do lists with ease, keeping your tasks synchronized across devices for personal or professional use.
- **Reclaim.ai**: An intelligent scheduling tool that prioritizes your time by automatically blocking periods for focused work, personal tasks, and breaks. It adapts to your routine, balancing meetings and uninterrupted work time.
- **Siri and Google Assistant**: Assistants that handle quick scheduling tasks, like creating appointments, checking conflicts, and syncing events across devices. Just say, *"Schedule a meeting tomorrow at 2 p.m.,"* and they'll handle the rest.
- **Zoom Integration with Calendly**: Combines Calendly's scheduling with automatic Zoom link generation, embedding meeting links directly in calendar invites to simplify virtual meetings.

These AI scheduling tools can save you tons of time and help you manage meetings more effectively, allowing you to focus on less tedious tasks. Let's put one of these tools into action with a hands-on exercise.

Hands-On Exercise: Streamlining Your Scheduling with Calendly

Complexity Rating: 2/5

Estimated Time: 10-15 minutes for initial setup; 2-5 minutes for future scheduling

In this exercise, you'll set up **Calendly** to make scheduling meetings easier than ever. This setup will allow others to book time with you based on your availability, and if you integrate **Zoom**, each meeting will come with a ready-to-use link for virtual sessions:

1. **Sign Up for Calendly and Sync Your Calendar:** Start by creating an account at **Calendly** and connecting it to your primary calendar, such as **Google Calendar**, **Apple Calendar**, **Outlook**. This sync ensures that Calendly automatically detects your availability and prevents double bookings.
2. **Define Your Availability**: Choose the days and times you are available for meetings, like Tuesdays and Thursdays from 10 a.m. to 3 p.m. Set specific durations for each meeting, such as 15, 30, or 60 minutes, so Calendly automatically blocks the right amount of time.
3. **Customize Your Meeting Types:** Create specific meeting types like *"Client Consultation"* or *"Team Check-In,"* and include short descriptions so invitees understand the purpose of each meeting. For virtual meetings, you can integrate your **Zoom** account to streamline scheduling.
    - Open **Calendly Settings**, navigate to the **Integrations** section, and select **Zoom**
    - Follow the prompts to connect your Zoom account

   - Once integrated, Calendly will automatically generate Zoom links for virtual meetings and include them in the invitations, saving you time and effort
4. **Share Your Calendly Link:** Copy your unique Calendly link, such as *"calendly.com/yourname,"* and share it with clients, colleagues, or anyone who needs to book time with you. Invitees will see only your available slots and can schedule a meeting that works for both of you.
5. **Set Up Automated Reminders and Notifications:** Turn on email or text reminders to ensure invitees show up for their meetings. Adjust your settings so you receive notifications when someone books a time on your calendar.
6. **Test the Setup:** Share your link with a friend or colleague to see how the process works from their side. Confirm that time slots, reminders, and meeting details (including Zoom links if applicable) function as expected.

By following these steps, you'll simplify your scheduling process and eliminate the back-and-forth of setting up meetings. Once Calendly is set up, scheduling becomes as easy as sharing a link, allowing you to focus on tasks without hassle.

Best Practices for Calendar Management with AI

To make the most of AI for your calendar management, consider these best practices:

- **Update your calendar regularly:** The more accurate and up-to-date your calendar is, the better your AI assistant will be at scheduling and managing your time.
- **Use recurring events:** When you have regular standing meetings or tasks, set them up as recurring events so that your assistant can handle them automatically.
- **Set buffer times:** Avoid back-to-back meetings by setting buffer times between events. AI tools like Reclaim.ai can automatically schedule time for breaks or focused work.

- **Take advantage of reminders:** Don't rely on your memory for essential tasks—use your virtual assistant to set reminders so you stay on top of your schedule without extra effort.

Using AI for calendar management isn't just about convenience—it's about freeing up your mental space. You can focus more on what truly needs your attention by automating mundane, everyday tasks like scheduling, setting reminders, and managing conflicts.

Key Takeaways:

- AI scheduling tools like **Calendly** and **Reclaim.ai** simplify scheduling by automating tasks such as finding meeting times, managing conflicts, and sending reminders.
- Integrating AI tools with your calendar ensures seamless time management, allowing you to focus on important tasks without the stress of manual updates.
- Best practices like updating your calendar, setting buffer times, and using recurring events maximize the efficiency of AI-powered tools while reducing scheduling hassles.

2.4 MANAGING YOUR MONEY SMARTER WITH AI

Managing personal finances can be a daunting task, especially when juggling multiple accounts, bills, and investments. Fortunately, AI can simplify the process, helping you stay organized and make smarter financial decisions. From budgeting to investing, AI-powered tools can offer personalized advice, automate your finances, and even provide real-time insights to help you meet your financial goals.

Just as we discussed how AI can boost efficiency by managing your to-dos or streamlining emails to save time, AI can be a game-changer in managing your money. Imagine how you can utilize powerful AI tools to automate your savings, track spending, and get tailored financial advice—all without a financial advisor.

Getting Started with AI Financial Tools

AI-driven personal finance tools simplify managing money and reduce stress. Whether you want to automate bill payments, track expenses, or optimize your investments, these tools are customized to your unique financial goals and lifestyle.

By leveraging data-driven insights, AI-powered platforms help you take control of your finances with minimal effort. From analyzing spending habits and recommending personalized savings strategies to making smarter investment decisions, these tools remove the guesswork and empower you to achieve financial health with confidence.

For example, you can automate your savings with tools like **Acorns**, which effortlessly invest spare change from everyday purchases. You can get a clearer picture of your financial situation by using **Empower,** which tracks your portfolio and helps you reduce fees and plan for long-term goals. If you're trying to get out of debt, build a savings cushion, or grow your wealth, these tools will provide you with the structure and guidance needed to stay on track.

Automating Your Financial Life

One of the most worthwhile features of AI in finance is its ability to streamline routine tasks through automation. Paying bills, transferring money into savings, or making regular investments can take up valuable time and mental energy. By using AI-driven tools to handle these tasks, your financial management is simplified and you ensure that critical actions occur on time.

Automation allows you to *"set it and forget it"* when it comes to tasks like moving money into savings or keeping track of bills and expenses. Knowing that your finances are taken care of, even when you're busy with other aspects of life, gives you peace of mind. You can think of it as having a personal assistant for your money, ensuring everything runs smoothly behind the scenes.

Financial Tools Worth Exploring:

- **PocketGuard**: PocketGuard simplifies budgeting by showing you exactly how much disposable income you have after covering bills, goals, and necessities. It connects to your bank accounts, categorizes spending automatically, and helps you stay within limits with its "In My Pocket" feature.
- **YNAB (You Need A Budget)**: This tool helps you allocate every dollar you earn towards a specific purpose, ensuring you stay on top of your budget. It also offers AI-powered financial forecasting based on your spending patterns.
- **Acorns**: Acorns automatically rounds up your purchases to the nearest dollar and invests the extra change. It's an excellent tool for beginner investors looking to grow their savings effortlessly.
- **Empower**: For those interested in managing investments, Empower offers AI tools that track your portfolio, analyze fees, and suggest strategies to improve your financial performance.

Now, we'll try out a hands-on exercise to see how easy it is to set up an automated system for tracking your spending and managing your budget.

Hands-On Exercise: Tracking Spending Habits with PocketGuard

Complexity Rating: 2/5

Estimated Time: 15-20 minutes for initial setup; 10-15 minutes per month to review summaries, adjust transactions, and update budgets

Let's dive into tracking your spending habits using **PocketGuard**. This is a good tool for getting a clear picture of where your money is going and how to optimize your budget:

1. **Sign Up for PocketGuard:** Create a PocketGuard account and follow the prompts to securely link your bank accounts, credit cards, and bills. The app will guide you through securely linking your bank accounts, credit cards, and bills to automatically track your finances.
2. **Set Up Spending Categories:** Once your accounts are linked, PocketGuard will automatically categorize your transactions into groups like groceries, dining, and utilities. Review these categories and manually adjust them as needed to match your spending habits and goals.
3. **Review "In My Pocket" Insights:** PocketGuard calculates your disposable income after accounting for bills, goals, and necessities. Use the *"In My Pocket"* feature to understand how much money is available for discretionary spending and to identify areas where you can cut back.
4. **Set Spending Limits:** Set limits for specific spending categories, such as dining or entertainment, to keep your budget on track. PocketGuard will help you stay within these limits by notifying you when you're nearing them.
5. **Monitor Your Financial Health:** Use PocketGuard's easy-to-read dashboard to track your monthly spending trends, review your progress toward financial goals, and make adjustments as needed.

Disclaimer: Privacy and Security Concerns

You may have concerns about linking your financial accounts to third-party services like PocketGuard. Understand that PocketGuard uses bank-level encryption and security protocols to protect your information. However, if you're uncomfortable sharing your data with third-party tools, consider using manual budgeting methods or tools that don't require account linking. Always review a service's privacy policy to ensure it aligns with your data sharing and storage comfort level.

Using tools like PocketGuard to track your spending habits isn't just a one-time fix—it's a habit that, when repeated, can create lasting financial change. As you monitor your expenses, you'll spot trends, find areas to cut back and understand where your money is going. Over time, this consistent tracking will give you the insights you need to make smarter financial decisions and adjust your habits to align with your goals.

The beauty of AI-powered financial tools is that they do much of the heavy lifting for you. Instead of manually calculating your budget or remembering to transfer money into savings, AI automates these processes for you. By putting more of your finances on autopilot, you'll have more time and mental energy to focus on achieving more significant financial objectives—such as planning for a major purchase, eliminating credit card debt, or increasing your long-term investments.

Now that you've seen how easy it is to start tracking your finances with AI, let's review some best practices to maximize the benefits of these tools.

Best Practices for Using AI to Manage Finances:

- **Link all accounts for a holistic view:** Connecting your accounts (checking, savings, credit cards, etc.) to a single AI tool will provide a comprehensive overview of your finances.
- **Set clear goals:** Whether you're saving for a vacation or paying off debt, defining your financial goals will help AI tools provide more accurate insights and recommendations.

- **Review and adjust regularly:** While AI can automate much of your financial management, you should continue to review your progress periodically and adjust as needed. Regular check-ins ensure that your finances stay aligned with your goals.
- **Stay vigilant for security:** Use strong passwords and two-factor authentication when using AI tools to protect your financial information.

Using AI for financial management makes your life easier and helps you make more informed decisions, guiding you toward savvy saving, spending, and investing habits. By allowing AI to manage the more tedious aspects of your finances, you can focus on bigger financial goals, knowing that the day-to-day money management is under control.

Key Takeaways:

- AI-powered financial tools can simplify budgeting, saving, and investing, offering personalized insights based on your habits.
- Automating your financial tasks—such as savings and bill payments—frees up mental energy and ensures you stay on track toward your financial goals.
- Regularly reviewing and adjusting your automated financial system ensures that AI is helping you meet your evolving financial needs.

2.5 STRESS-FREE TRAVEL PLANNING USING AI

Now that you're tracking your expenses and setting budgets, it's time to focus on something lighter and more fun—planning a trip! Travel planning can be exciting, but with so many choices for flights, hotels, and activities, it can quickly become overwhelming. Fortunately, AI-powered tools streamline the process by offering personalized recommendations, real-time updates, and price predictions to help you get the best deals. Whether you're a seasoned traveler or planning your first big trip, AI tools make every step—from booking to itinerary management—simpler and more efficient.

AI-Powered Travel Tools for Smarter Planning

AI-powered travel tools take the guesswork out of planning. Tools like **Hopper** and **Google Travel** use AI algorithms to analyze historical pricing data and predict price changes, helping you book flights and hotels at the best rates. Hopper, for example, notifies you when prices are expected to rise or drop, while Google Travel provides insights on price trends, empowering you to make informed booking decisions.

Streamlining the Booking Process

After finding the best deals, AI tools like **Skyscanner** and **Kayak** streamline booking by comparing prices across multiple platforms. This saves you the hassle of manually checking different sites for the lowest prices. Additionally, these platforms help handle last-minute changes or cancellations. If a flight is canceled, AI travel assistants can suggest alternative flights or automatically rebook you based on your schedule.

Itinerary Planning with AI

Once your trip is booked, AI can help organize every detail of your itinerary. Tools like **TripIt** and **Google Travel** compile all your travel information—from flights to hotel bookings—into a single, easy-to-navigate location. Instead of juggling confirmation emails or multiple apps, these platforms create a well-organized itinerary that's accessible with just a few taps.

But AI goes well beyond just compiling your trip details and actually tailors your itinerary to your preferences. For example, some AI-powered tools will ask for your input on additional preferences after syncing your travel reservations to create an even more customized travel experience. They may inquire about your interests, such as:

- **Types of Activities**: Whether you're interested in outdoor adventures, cultural experiences, or family-friendly activities, AI can suggest local attractions based on your preference.

- **Preferred Travel Pace:** Do you prefer a packed schedule or more downtime between activities? AI can adjust your itinerary to ensure you're not overwhelmed while still making the most of your trip.
- **Cuisine Preferences:** If food is a meaningful part of your travel experience, AI can recommend restaurants according to your tastes, whether you're looking for fine dining, local street food, or specific cuisines.
- **Budget Considerations:** AI can suggest activities or restaurants that fit your budget, ensuring you don't overspend while still enjoying the best your destination has to offer.
- **Optimized Routes**: AI can map out the most efficient route by grouping nearby activities and minimizing travel time so you can make the most of each day.

With AI, your trip becomes a curated experience that matches your interests and allows for flexibility and real-time updates. From tourist hotspots to hidden gems, AI-generated itineraries help you travel efficiently without the stress of manual planning.

Travel Assistance and Support

The power of AI doesn't stop once you arrive at your destination. AI travel assistants are there to provide ongoing support *during* your trip, too. For example, TripIt offers instant updates and reminders on flight statuses, tracks any changes to your itinerary, and helps you organize your travel plans efficiently. If you encounter a flight delay, you can count on your AI assistant to immediately suggest alternative routes or rebook your travel arrangements without you having to navigate the process manually. It's like having a personal travel concierge at your fingertips, ready to assist with disruptions or last-minute changes.

Now, you can appreciate a smoother travel experience, allowing you to focus on enjoying your holiday rather than worrying about the logistics.

Suggested Tools for Streamlining Travel Planning

These AI-powered tools help make travel planning smoother, more efficient, and tailored to your preferences. Whether you're booking flights, organizing itineraries, or handling last-minute changes, these tools offer personalized support for all your travel needs:

- **Google Travel**: Assists with managing bookings, itineraries, and travel recommendations, with features like price tracking and personalized suggestions.
- **Hopper**: Predicts flight and hotel price fluctuations and notifies you of the best time to book.
- **Kayak**: Scans multiple travel booking sites instantly for flights, hotels, and car rentals.
- **Skyscanner**: Compares prices across multiple platforms to help you find the best travel deals.
- **TripIt**: Automatically organizes your travel itinerary by compiling details from your confirmation emails.

Using these AI tools allows travelers to enjoy more seamless, stress-free experiences from the booking stage to real-time assistance during their trips.

Hands-On Exercise: Planning a Trip with AI

Complexity Rating: 2/5

Estimated Time: 15-30 minutes

In this exercise, we'll focus on creating a personalized travel itinerary using AI-powered tools so you can see firsthand how AI helps plan each part of your trip.

1. **Choose Your Itinerary Planning Tool:** Select an AI-powered tool like **TripIt** or **Google Travel** to begin. If you haven't used these before, sign up and explore their features.
2. **Input Your Destination and Interests:** Enter the location you're visiting and the types of activities you're interested in. For example, TripIt may reference details from your email if you've already booked flights or hotels, while Google Travel lets you specify interests like *"museums," "nature,"* or *"food tours."*
3. **Set Your Preferences for Travel Pace and Budget:** Most AI itinerary tools allow you to tailor your schedule. Indicate whether you prefer a relaxed pace with fewer activities or a jam-packed schedule. Include your trip budget to receive recommendations that fit within your financial plan.
4. **Generate a Sample Itinerary:** Based on your inputs, the AI tool will create a suggested itinerary. Review the itinerary and note how activities are grouped by location, cutting down on travel time and making your day more efficient.
5. **Customize and Optimize Your Plan:** Take a few minutes to refine the itinerary. Add or remove activities based on your interests, adjust the schedule to match your energy levels, and confirm that the suggestions align with your goals for the trip. You can also use the tool to set reminders or add notes for specific times.
6. **Save and Access Your Itinerary on the Go:** Once you're happy with the itinerary, save it in the app and download it for offline access (if this feature is offered). This way, you can easily follow your plan without needing constant internet access.

By following these steps, you'll experience how AI can streamline trip planning, create a structured itinerary, and allow you to focus on enjoying your journey instead of worrying about logistics. Now, if only AI could pack our suitcases for us...

Key Takeaways:

- Track airfare fluctuations and get notified when it's the best time to book, ensuring you save money on travel with tools like **Hopper** and **GoogleTravel**.
- Compare prices across multiple platforms and quickly secure the best travel deals using **Skyscanner** without manually visiting different websites.
- Use **TripIt** to streamline your travel planning by automatically organizing itineraries from confirmation emails while also receiving real-time flight updates and managing last-minute changes with ease.

3

GENERATIVE AI

Create Like Never Before

Now that we've explored AI's practical side, let's tap into its creative potential.

3.1 GENERATIVE AI UNLEASHED: WHAT IT CAN DO FOR YOU

Picture a tool that can generate ideas, compose music, or create artwork—all from a simple prompt that you provide. This is the potential of **generative AI**, a rapidly advancing technology that makes high-quality content accessible to everyone. Generative AI will bring your ideas to life with just a few clicks or word commands.

But what exactly is generative AI? Simply put, it's artificial intelligence designed to create new content—such as text, images, or music—by learning from existing data. Unlike traditional AI, which focuses on analyzing data and making predictions, generative AI produces original work. Think of it like an artist creating a masterpiece inspired by their knowledge of countless artworks.

What makes this so exciting is that generative AI opens up endless possibilities for anyone looking to expand their creativity. Here are some of the most empowering benefits it can bring to your creative process:

- **Speed and Efficiency**: Generative AI allows you to produce high-quality content in a fraction of the time it would take manually. Whether you're drafting an article, designing a logo, or composing music, AI speeds up the process, making it easier to bring your ideas quickly to life.
- **Enhanced Creativity**: In many cases, AI can provide new ideas or creative solutions you may not think of on your own. It can help you explore new perspectives and push your artistic boundaries.
- **Automation of Repetitive Tasks**: For creative professionals, repetitive tasks can take up valuable time. Generative AI takes over these tedious activities, such as drafting multiple product descriptions or creating basic design mockups, letting you focus on more in-depth creative work.

Throughout this chapter, we'll explore how generative AI is and can be used for different projects like text generation, visual art, and music. Let's begin with text generation—an accessible and handy starting point for beginners.

Re-Introducing ChatGPT for Generative AI

So far, we've witnessed ChatGPT simplify tasks, automate workflows, and boost productivity. While these practical uses have made our day-to-day tasks easier, we've only scratched the surface of what AI can do. Now, we'll continue to unlock more of ChatGPT's potential as a creative partner capable of bringing your ideas to life through unique content generation.

Let's say you need to write a blog post about the benefits of remote work. To kickstart your writing, you can prompt ChatGPT with, "*Write a blog post about the benefits of remote work.*" Within seconds, you'll have a solid draft ready for refinement. ChatGPT's role as an inventive collaborator helps you shape and polish ideas, allowing you to produce professional-quality work—even if writing isn't your expertise.

How does it do this? Generative AI tools like ChatGPT don't just follow predefined rules; they learn patterns from vast ranges of text-based language data to create something fresh with each prompt. When you give ChatGPT a prompt, it doesn't pull from pre-written text; it generates responses based on the patterns it has learned. The result? Content that's unique, adaptable, and feels crafted just for you. This ability to respond creatively makes ChatGPT a dynamic tool for brainstorming, drafting, and exploring ideas in a natural and collaborative way, empowering beginners and experts alike.

Hands-On Exercise: Generating Content with ChatGPT

Complexity Rating: 2/5

Estimated Time: 15-20 minutes

Let's get imaginative and use **ChatGPT** to create a product description for a fictional, quirky item. This exercise will show how generative AI can be a creative partner in crafting unique, engaging content that is worthy of publishing.

1. **Choose a Fictional Product Idea:** Brainstorm a fun, fictional product with a unique twist. Try something whimsical or unusual—like *"an umbrella that changes color based on your mood"* or *"sneakers that make you jump higher."* Let your creativity shine; there are no wrong answers here!
2. **Input Your Prompt:** Once you have a fictional product in mind, open ChatGPT and type a prompt describing it. For instance, try: *"Write a product description for sneakers that make you jump higher, including key features and benefits."*
3. **Review the Output:** Look at the product description ChatGPT generates. Does it capture the fun and quirky nature of your product? Look for details that make the product feel unique and exciting. Remember, ChatGPT is your creative partner, providing you with a foundation upon which you can build.
4. **Refine and Personalize:** Adjust the description to match your style. Add details if necessary or request more

information, such as "*Describe the materials these sneakers are made of*" or "*Who is the target market for these sneakers?*"

5. **Expand the Description:** If you want to go further, ask ChatGPT for additional creative elements, such as a catchy tagline or marketing suggestions. This step will demonstrate how AI can do more than just generate text—it can inspire full marketing ideas.

By the end of this exercise, you'll have a playful and unique product description that's ready to use, demonstrating how AI can transform your imaginative ideas into engaging, well-structured content. Generative AI provides a solid creative foundation, taking the pressure off the blank page and allowing you to focus on adding your personal touch. With AI as a collaborator, you can bring your vision to life while making the final product truly your own.

Key Takeaways:

- **Generative AI** brings new opportunities to explore creativity, with tools like **ChatGPT** that help users quickly generate and develop written content.
- By speeding up the creative process, generative AI allows you to produce drafts and refine ideas in minutes, giving you more time to personalize and perfect your work.
- ChatGPT is a supportive collaborator in creativity, helping with brainstorming, drafting, and polishing content that makes creative work more accessible for everyone, from beginners to seasoned professionals.

3.2 SUPERCHARGING YOUR CREATIVITY WITH AI

Now that we've explored how **generative AI** can craft written content let's further examine its role as a brainstorming partner. Beyond producing polished content, AI can help you overcome creative blocks and spark fresh ideas. If you've ever found yourself looking at a blank page or felt stalled on a project, generative AI can step in—not to replace your creativity but to offer new ideas, unexpected solutions, and fresh perspectives. This creative assistant can help you gather inspiration, unlock possibilities, and provide the momentum to keep you moving forward.

Overcoming Creative Blocks with AI

Getting started or breaking through a block are two of the biggest challenges in any creative process. Whether you're writing, designing, or brainstorming ideas, generative AI can help you push through those barriers.

Say you're writing a blog post but struggling to organize your thoughts. Instead of getting stuck, you can input your general idea into a tool like ChatGPT, which will generate potential outlines or headings to assist with your process. From there, you can adapt those suggestions, turning AI-generated concepts into something that's uniquely yours.

Similarly, if you're developing a concept for a new product or business idea but aren't sure how to expand it, AI tools can suggest new angles or features you might be unaware of. Imagine having a creative companion ready to offer fresh ideas anytime!

By using AI to break through mental roadblocks, you can generate content faster and avoid the frustration of wondering where to begin.

Hands-On Exercise: Brainstorming with ChatGPT

Complexity Rating: 1/5

Estimated Time: 10-15 minutes

Let's get practical by using **ChatGPT** as a brainstorming tool. For this exercise, we'll focus on generating ideas to help kickstart a creative project:

1. **Pick a Creative Project**: Choose a project you're working on or want to start. It could be anything—writing a short story, designing a logo, brainstorming a business idea, or planning an event.
2. **Input a Broad Prompt**: Open **ChatGPT** and start with a broad, open-ended prompt to get some initial ideas. For

example, if you're writing a story, you might say, *"Generate five unique character ideas for a fantasy novel."* If you're designing a logo, you could prompt, *"Suggest five color schemes for a modern, minimalist logo."*

3. **Refine the Prompt:** Once you have a few initial ideas, refine the prompt to get more specific. This step helps you focus on the details that matter most. For example, ask ChatGPT to help develop a character or dig deeper into a particular idea: *"Expand on the character [insert name], and describe her backstory and personality."* This back-and-forth pattern is vital—adjusting the prompts will guide ChatGPT toward the exact ideas you need.
4. **Use the Generated Ideas as a Starting Point**: AI-generated concepts can act as a springboard for your own creativity. Adjust them, add your unique twist, or build them into something new.

With this exercise, you'll come away with a range of fresh ideas—ones you may not have imagined without AI's support. Notice the rhythm: start with a prompt, review the output, and refine it, bringing each result closer to your vision. This back-and-forth flow lets you guide ChatGPT, generating more focused and valuable ideas along the way. Remember, this exercise isn't necessarily about creating a finished product; it's about sparking inspiration and shaping your next creative step. And with AI's speed, you can generate and refine ideas in a fraction of the time, allowing you to focus on developing the ones that resonate most.

Key Takeaways:

- AI can help you generate new ideas and perspectives when facing creative blocks, offering a fresh approach to problem-solving.
- **Generative AI** tools like **ChatGPT** can assist in brainstorming for writing, design, or other imaginative projects, providing a starting point for you to build upon.

- Using AI as a collaborative brainstorming tool can speed up your ideation process while infusing the final product with your creativity and style.

3.3 CREATING ART WITH GENERATIVE AI: A BEGINNER'S GUIDE

Generative AI's versatility makes it a powerful tool for nearly any creative endeavor. While we've explored **ChatGPT's** text generation, let's expand into the visual realm and see how generative AI tools like **DALL-E** allow for effortless artistic creation. These tools aren't just for writers or coders; they're designed to help anyone create new content across various mediums, from text and images to music and design. By recognizing patterns in large sets of data, AI can interpret your prompts and produce original content—bringing your ideas to life in unique and exciting ways.

Bringing Visual Concepts to Life with DALL-E

Just as ChatGPT assists with writing, tools like DALL-E make it easy to transform your ideas into visual form. Accessible through **OpenAI's** website, DALL-E enables anyone to generate professional-quality images from simple prompts, opening creative opportunities for those without formal art training or design software. Imagine describing *"a surreal landscape with floating mountains and glowing trees"* and watching that vision materialize within seconds. DALL-E makes experimenting with self-expression easy, whether you're interested in realistic portraits, abstract art, or anything in between.

DALL-E's interface is intuitive, offering you a flexible platform to experiment with different artistic styles and concepts. You can refine your results by specifying details like lighting, colors, and focal points. This process allows you to personalize each image so that your vision is accurately reflected. For instance, instead of simply requesting a *"cozy coffee shop,"* you could try something more specific, like *"a cozy coffee shop on a rainy day, with warm lighting, people sitting by the window, and a barista making coffee behind the counter."* This added detail helps DALL-E generate an image closely aligned with your intent.

Key Benefits of DALL-E:

- **Accessibility**: DALL-E puts high-quality visual creation within reach for everyone, eliminating the need for advanced design skills or specialized software.
- **Creative Freedom**: DALL-E's versatility allows you to experiment with various artistic styles and concepts, from realistic to surreal, fostering open-ended exploration.
- **Speed**: With DALL-E, generating images is nearly instantaneous, enabling rapid testing, iteration, and refinement of creative ideas.
- **Customization**: Detailed prompts enhance DALL-E's ability to create images that reflect your unique vision, with options to adjust elements like colors, lighting, and style.
- **Inspiration**: By interpreting your prompts in unexpected ways, DALL-E can spark new ideas and artistic directions, encouraging broader creative exploration.
- **Cost-Effectiveness**: DALL-E provides an affordable alternative to expensive design tools, making custom visuals accessible on a budget.

A Note on DALL-E's Limitations

Though DALL-E offers remarkable creative potential, certain limitations may impact specific projects. Here's what to keep in mind for generating the best results:

- **Complex or Technical Designs**: DALL-E excels in artistic expression rather than precision, so it may struggle with detailed technical requests, like blueprints or mechanical designs.
- **Human Faces**: Highly realistic faces may appear distorted or include unusual features, making it less reliable for portrait-style images.
- **Text in Images**: Incorporating legible written text in DALL-E-generated images can be challenging, as text often appears distorted or unclear.

- **Scale and Precision**: DALL-E is not ideal for designs requiring exact proportions or measurements, like architectural renderings.
- **Overly Detailed Prompts**: Providing too much information at once may confuse the AI; focusing on one or two main elements typically yields the best results.

Understanding DALL-E's strengths and limits can help you use it more effectively across diverse creative projects, giving you a clear framework for getting the most out of this innovative tool.

Hands-On Exercise: Creating Art with DALL-E

Complexity Rating: 2/5

Estimated Time: 15-20 minutes

Now it's your turn to create visually stunning artwork with **DALL-E**! The great news is that since you're already using ChatGPT, you can access DALL-E seamlessly without any extra setup. Simply type your request as a prompt, and the platform will generate your image. Follow these steps to explore the power and flexibility of AI art creation:

1. **Choose a Concept**: Start by thinking of what you'd like to create. You'll want a clear idea of whether it's something realistic or imaginative. For example:
   - *"A peaceful beach at sunrise"*
   - *"A bustling, futuristic city at night"*
   - *"A surreal desert with floating islands"*
   - *"A magical forest with glowing plants"*
2. **Define the Art Style**: To get more precise results, specify the artistic style you'd like the AI to use. Here are some styles you can experiment with:
   - **Sketch**: *"Create a pencil sketch of a mountain landscape"*
   - **Line Drawing**: *"A minimalist line drawing of a cat"*
   - **Watercolor**: *"A watercolor painting of a sunset over the ocean"*
   - **Oil Painting**: *"An oil painting of a historic castle on a hill"*
   - **3D Render**: *"A 3D render of a futuristic spacecraft"*

- **Abstract**: *"An abstract painting of swirling colors representing emotions"*

3. **Write a Descriptive Prompt**: Open **DALL-E** and type a clear, detailed prompt. Combining your concept and style, you could say:
   - *"A peaceful beach at sunrise with soft waves and a lighthouse in the background, in watercolor style"*
   - *"A futuristic city at night with neon lights and flying cars, in a 3D render"*
   - *"A magical forest with glowing plants and a river, in oil painting style"*
   - *"A surreal desert with floating islands and two moons in the sky, sketched in black and white"*
4. **Generate the Image**: Click to generate the image and review the result. Is it what you envisioned? Remember that you can continually refine the prompt to get closer to your ideal image.
5. **Refine and Adjust**: If the result isn't exactly what you want, here are a few ways to refine your prompts:
   - Add specific colors: *"A watercolor painting of a sunset with vibrant pinks and oranges in the sky"*
   - Specify the lighting: *"An oil painting of a historic castle illuminated by moonlight"*
   - Include focal points: *"A line drawing of a cat sitting by a window with a plant in the background"*
6. **Explore Variations**: After generating your image, explore different variations. DALL-E allows you to regenerate the same prompt with slight adjustments. For example:
   - *"Add a sunset in the background"*
   - *"Make the waves more prominent and reduce the number of clouds"*
   - *"Increase the contrast between the neon lights and the buildings"*

By the end of this exercise, you'll have created your very own AI-generated artwork that reflects your vision. The beauty of AI art creation is that it's a collaborative process between your imagination and the tool's capabilities—refining prompts allows you to bring your ideas to life in exciting ways.

Beyond Basic Image Creation

While **DALL-E** is a fantastic starting point for creating unique visuals, other AI art tools offer additional capabilities worth exploring as you become more comfortable. For example:

- **MidJourney**: If you're ready to push your creative boundaries further, MidJourney is a fantastic option. Known for producing more imaginative, surreal imagery, MidJourney allows you to create experimental and artistic visuals that stand out.
- **Runway ML**: A tool that enhances creative workflows by using AI to generate new visuals, 3D elements, and video content, perfect for creators working on multimedia projects.
- **Artbreeder**: A tool that allows you to create unique images by combining different artistic styles, faces, or landscapes. Artbreeder uses AI to generate new visuals based on user inputs, ideal for designers and artists looking for inspiration.

As you explore these tools, you'll see how AI art can complement and expand your creative workflow. Whether designing social media content, creating visual assets for your business, or simply exploring art as a hobby, generative AI helps you go beyond the limitations of your artistic skills and brings your ideas to life.

Key Takeaways:

- **AI allows you to create high-quality, unique visuals**: Tools like **DALL-E** enable anyone to produce impressive artwork with a single prompt, making creativity accessible and attainable.

- **Generative AI refines your ideas**: You can create AI-generated images that match your exact vision by providing detailed prompts and adjusting the results. The more specific and thoughtful your prompts, the more impressive and tailored your results will be.
- **Explore advanced tools for imaginative visuals**: As you gain confidence, experiment with platforms like **MidJourney** to push the boundaries of your creative work.

4

ADVANCING AS A MODERN PROFESSIONAL WITH AI

AI is rapidly transforming how we work, making our jobs easier and creating new opportunities across various industries. In fact, AI and automation are anticipated to generate countless new job opportunities as advancements continue, even as some roles evolve or are phased out. From automating mundane tasks to enhancing creativity, AI is reshaping the workforce, making many roles more strategic and intellectually stimulating. The shift isn't about AI taking over—it's about professionals taking advantage of AI to unlock greater productivity and efficiency, allowing them to focus on higher-level thinking and problem-solving.

In this chapter, we'll explore how AI tools can help you enhance your career, streamline your business, and make wiser business decisions, allowing work to be more engaging and fulfilling overall.

4.1 CRAFTING A RESUME THAT GETS NOTICED

Crafting the perfect resume can seem like an overwhelming challenge, especially when you're tailoring it to multiple job descriptions. Thankfully, AI can simplify this process, helping you format your resume for maximum impact and customize it to catch the attention of both hiring managers and **Applicant Tracking Systems (ATS).**

Leveraging AI for Professional Resumes

With the right AI tools, creating a resume becomes less about formatting headaches and more about showcasing your unique skills and experience. AI-powered platforms like **Resume.io** take the guesswork out of structuring your resume, offering pre-designed templates highlighting the essential elements—such as work experience, education, and skills—while keeping the layout clean and professional. AI resume tools can significantly affect how your resume is received, especially when hiring managers are reviewing hundreds of applications.

But AI doesn't stop at formatting. These tools also help match your resume to specific job descriptions, increasing the odds of your application passing ATS filters and making it to the hiring manager's desk. By scanning job postings for specific keywords and aligning your resume with the language used by employers, AI ensures your resume will stand out to both humans and machines.

Enhancing Resume Content with AI

Beyond formatting and employer matching, AI can enhance the actual content within your resume. Tools like **Grammarly** and **QuillBot** optimize your language, refining grammar and style to make your resume clear, concise, and error-free. Grammarly can also highlight opportunities to make your writing more compelling and polished. At the same time, QuillBot can help rephrase awkward sentences or overly complicated language, assuring that your resume is not only ATS-compatible but also impressive to human readers.

As many companies in today's competitive job market rely on ATS to screen for certain keywords and formatting standards, you can optimize your resume for these systems, ensuring it passes the initial screening. For instance, it will enhance your bullet points to better reflect the qualifications and experience required for the job. Optimizing your resume doesn't just help with ATS either—it ensures that your resume stands out and grabs the attention of hiring managers by emphasizing relevant skills, work experience, and accomplishments.

Balancing Automation with Personalization

While AI can automate many aspects of resume creation, it's essential to strike the right balance between automation and personalization. AI can format your resume and optimize its content, but adding personal touches—like specific achievements or anecdotal examples—will set you apart from other candidates. Your contributions and unique experiences make your resume stand out in a sea of applications, so sprinkle in elements that highlight your individuality and professional journey.

Additionally, it is highly recommended that you regularly update your resume with AI-driven insights. Job descriptions constantly evolve, and the most in-demand skills tend to shift over time. AI can scan job postings and recommend certain skills to highlight or areas that need updating. Your resume should remain current and competitive, especially in rapidly changing industries like healthcare, technology, and finance.

Build Your Standout Resume Using AI Tools

The tools listed below are designed to simplify resume creation and ensure your resume stands out by optimizing content for ATS systems and human readers alike. Whether you're looking to improve formatting, enhance language, or tailor your resume for specific job applications, these AI-powered tools can help.

- **Grammarly:** An AI-powered writing assistant that ensures your resume is polished and professional by correcting grammar, punctuation, and style while enhancing clarity and tone.
- **Jobscan**: A tool designed to optimize your resume for Applicant Tracking Systems (ATS) by comparing your resume

to the job description and recommending keywords and adjustments.

- **QuillBot**: A tool to help you rephrase and improve awkward or overly complicated sentences in your resume, making it more concise and readable.
- **Resume.io**: A familiar AI-powered resume builder offering professional templates for various industries, helping you easily structure and format your resume.
- **Zety**: Another AI-driven resume builder with templates designed to meet different professional needs, simplifying the creation of an ATS-friendly resume.

Hands-On Exercise: Using AI to Build a Standout Resume

Complexity Rating: 2/5

Estimated Time: 20-30 minutes

Follow these steps to experience how AI can help you create, update, or optimize your resume, making this crucial part of the job application process more efficient:

1. **Choose an AI Resume Tool**: Select an AI-powered resume builder, like **Resume.io** or **Zety.** These tools offer different templates for various industries and professional levels, allowing you to pick one that best suits your style and job market.
2. **Input Your Information**: Enter your details, including name, contact information, and professional summary. Next, input your work experience, education, and skills. Many AI tools automatically format this information into a clear and professional layout.
3. **Optimize for ATS**: Review the job description for the position you're applying for. Use keywords from the job listing and ensure your experience aligns with the required or recommended qualifications. AI tools can help by scanning job

descriptions and highlighting the primary terms you should include in your resume.

4. **Refine**: After structuring your resume and adding the relevant content, run it through a tool like **Grammarly** or **QuillBot**. These AI tools will check for grammar, tone, and style improvements, ensuring your resume reads smoothly and professionally.
5. **Customize for Each Job Application**: AI tools can also help you tailor your resume for different positions. Use these tools to quickly adjust your resume based on specific job requirements, adding or tweaking details to align with each application.

By the end of this exercise, you'll have a professional, ATS-friendly resume that showcases your skills and experience in the best possible light.

Key Takeaways:

- **Build an AI-enhanced resume easily**: Tools like **Resume.io** and **Zety** simplify the formatting and structuring of resumes, ensuring your document is clear and professional.
- **Enhance your resume content with AI**: Tools like **Grammarly** and **QuillBot** optimize grammar, tone, and style, making your resume more compelling to both **ATS** and human readers.
- **Stay competitive by updating regularly**: AI can scan job descriptions and suggest updates to your resume, ensuring it remains aligned with current job market demands.
- **Balance automation with personal touches**: While AI can handle formatting and keyword optimization, make your resume really stand out by adding your unique accomplishments.

4.2 WRITING AND EDITING WITH AI: GET YOUR MESSAGE ACROSS WITH EASE

Now that your resume is polished and ready to showcase your skills, it's time to focus on another crucial aspect of professional communication: clear and compelling writing. Whether you're drafting a business proposal, composing an email to a client, or writing a report, the quality of your writing can have a profound effect on how your message is received. That's where AI steps in—helping you create polished, effective documents in less time and with

Earlier in this book, we explored how generative AI supports the creative process—brainstorming ideas, drafting content, and helping you get started. But once your ideas are on the page, the next challenge is refining them. That's where AI editing tools step in: they focus on polishing your work, optimizing for clarity, professionalism, and impact. Think of it this way—generative AI helps you start strong, while editing AI ensures you finish with a polished, well-structured result. In this section, we'll focus on how these tools can transform rough drafts into clear, professional documents, whether it's an email, report, or proposal.

AI for Professional Writing

AI tools like **Grammarly** and **Hemingway** have become invaluable assistants in writing and editing professional documents. These tools ensure your work is free from spelling and grammatical errors while enhancing the clarity, tone, and impact of your message. Imagine having an expert editor on call who makes it easy for you to produce high-quality work, even under tight deadlines.

Grammarly, which we've covered in the previous section, doesn't just catch typos; it offers real-time suggestions to improve sentence structure, tone, and even the flow of your writing. It detects overly complex sentences, suggests easier-to-read alternatives, and ensures your tone is appropriate for your audience. Whether you're writing a quick email or a long-form report, Grammarly can refine your message and make it more compelling.

(Here's a little secret: I used Grammarly while writing this book and found its suggestions invaluable for refining my message and keeping the tone just right.)

Hemingway, on the other hand, is perfect for streamlining your content. If you use complex sentences or have a habit of passive writing, Hemingway will highlight these areas and offer suggestions to simplify and improve readability. For those drafting executive summaries or reports that must be concise and influential, Hemingway ensures you communicate clearly and without unnecessary jargon.

Editing for Clarity and Impact

One of the greatest strengths of AI writing tools is their ability to edit for clarity and impact. Take business proposals, for example. These documents are often dry and filled with dense information. However, AI suggestions can break down complex ideas into digestible, reader-friendly sentences, ensuring the flow of the document keeps the reader's attention.

Imagine you're writing a proposal to pitch a new product. Instead of spending hours refining every sentence, AI can suggest alternatives to improve the tone and persuasiveness of your writing. The result? A more articulate and engaging proposal that's more likely to make an impact on your audience.

Maintaining Consistency Across Documents

Consistency is fundamental in professional writing, especially for documents that are addressed to clients or stakeholders. AI tools ensure that your tone, terminology, and formatting remain consistent throughout your work. This cohesiveness is particularly useful for businesses where multiple people contribute to a single document or report.

For instance, Grammarly offers a style guide feature that allows you to set specific writing rules, such as preferred terminology or formatting guidelines. Every document should follow your company's standards, creating a unified, professional voice. Consistency in this way doesn't just make your documents look good or sound better—it builds trust and reliability with your audience.

Tools for Writing and Editing with AI

These AI-powered tools help streamline the writing and editing process, making it easier to create clear, compelling, and polished content. Whether using these tools for grammar corrections, tone adjustments, or improving readability, they ensure your documents are professional and effective:

- **Grammarly**: This tool refines your writing by correcting grammar, punctuation, and style while offering suggestions to enhance clarity and tone. Ideal for professional communication, emails, and reports.
- **Hemingway**: Hemingway helps simplify complex sentences, improve readability, and eliminate passive voice, making your writing more direct and easier to understand.
- **QuillBot**: Although less prominently mentioned, QuillBot can be used alongside Grammarly to help rephrase sentences, making them more concise and improving

---

Hands-On Exercise: Polishing a LinkedIn Profile Summary

Complexity Rating: 2/5

Estimated Time: 15-20 minutes

Your LinkedIn profile summary is your digital elevator pitch, and using AI can help you craft a clear, compelling message that showcases your professional strengths. Let's walk through how to create and polish a LinkedIn summary using **ChatGPT**, **Grammarly**, and **Hemingway**:

1. **Generate Your LinkedIn Profile Summary with ChatGPT:** Open **ChatGPT** and briefly describe your career, major achievements, and skills. Use a prompt like:

- *"Write a professional and engaging LinkedIn profile summary for a [your job title or desired role] with [number] years of experience. Highlight my key skills, accomplishments, and areas of expertise, such as [list specific skills]. Include a tone that is [your preferred tone, e.g., friendly, professional, or ambitious], and make it appealing to potential employers or connections in the [type of industry] industry. End with a statement that reflects my passion for [your passion, e.g., helping brands grow or leveraging data to drive decisions]."*
- ChatGPT will generate a well-rounded profile summary based on the information you provide. Here are some extra tips to guide your input:
  - **Be specific** about your expertise (e.g., *"data-driven marketer focusing on growing brand engagement"*).
  - **Highlight notable accomplishments** (e.g., *"helped increase brand awareness by 30% through targeted campaigns"*).
  - **Keep it concise** yet informative.

2. **Review with Grammarly:** Copy the summary generated by ChatGPT and paste it into **Grammarly**. Grammarly will help refine grammar, punctuation, tone, and sentence clarity. Pay special attention to:
   - **Tone Consistency:** Ensure the summary maintains a professional yet approachable tone.
   - **Active Voice:** Use Grammarly's suggestions to convert passive voice into active voice where applicable (e.g., "*led campaigns*" instead of "*was responsible for campaigns*").
   - **Clarity and Precision:** Look for areas where the summary is too vague or unclear, and adjust it based on Grammarly's suggestions.
3. **Refine with Hemingway:** Next, copy the updated text into **Hemingway**. This tool helps simplify the language and makes it more reader-friendly, which is ideal for a LinkedIn summary where brevity is key. Hemingway will:
   - **Highlight complex sentences** that need simplification. Break these down to make your profile easier to skim.

    - **Spot passive voice:** Ensure that the summary is as direct as possible.
    - **Suggest readability improvements:** LinkedIn summaries should be clear and easy to digest for a broad audience, including recruiters.
4. **Enhance Your Summary with Personal Touches:** Once you've run your profile through Grammarly and Hemingway, it's time to add a personal touch. Consider the following suggestions:
    - **Include a call to action:** Invite connections or recruiters to engage with you, such as: *"Feel free to connect with me if you're looking for a strategic marketer with a passion for brand growth and creative problem-solving."*
    - **Highlight your values and passions:** Personalize the summary by mentioning what drives you professionally, like: *"I'm passionate about creating data-driven strategies that grow brands and engage communities."*
    - **Add career goals:** Share what you're currently aiming to achieve in your career: *"Currently, I'm seeking new opportunities to lead innovative campaigns that push the boundaries of digital marketing."*
5. **Final Review and Personalization:** Revisit the final summary and make sure it reflects your professional expertise and personality. Consider whether the language sounds like *you* and if it aligns with the direction of your career. Ask yourself:
    - Does the summary highlight my notable achievements and skills?
    - Is the tone professional but approachable?
    - Is there a clear call to action or invitation to connect?

By the end of this exercise, you will have a polished, engaging LinkedIn summary that captures your professional strengths clearly and concisely. You will also see firsthand how AI tools like ChatGPT, Grammarly, and Hemingway can help refine your message and make it more appealing to potential employers or connections.

Best Practices for Writing with AI

Here's how to get the most out of editing AI tools while ensuring your unique voice still shines through:

- **Balance Automation with Personal Touches**: While AI tools optimize clarity and grammar, adding your own insights and tone is essential, especially in client communications or creative writing. AI won't know the nuances of your personal or brand voice, so always review the final content.
- **Use AI as a Continuous Learning Tool**: By reviewing the recurring suggestions from AI tools, you can learn to improve your writing habits. You may use passive voice too often or overcomplicate sentences. Over time, these AI insights can help you become a more efficient writer without requiring constant assistance.
- **Customize the Tool to Fit Your Needs**: Many AI editing platforms allow you to customize style preferences. Make use of this feature to maintain brand consistency. For example, set formal vs. informal communication rules, and define the keywords or core phrases your team or company should use.

Key Takeaways:

- **AI tools like Grammarly and Hemingway improve the clarity, tone, and grammar of your writing**: These tools make editing faster and more efficient, ensuring your message is professional and polished.
- **Using AI for editing helps ensure consistency**: You can maintain a unified tone and style across your documents, especially for teams collaborating on a project.
- **AI-driven edits enhance the impact of your writing**: By improving readability and clarity, AI ensures your content resonates with your audience, helping you communicate more effectively.

By utilizing AI for writing and editing, you can streamline the final stages of content creation and ensure that every piece you create is clear, consistent, and captivating for your audience. While generative AI gets the ball rolling, editing AI helps you cross the finish line with polished, attention-grabbing content.

4.3 GENERATING SOCIAL MEDIA CONTENT WITHOUT THE HASSLE

In today's digital landscape, keeping your social media channels fresh and engaging can feel like a full-time job. As we've seen, AI offers powerful solutions across many aspects of professional life—from writing to editing. Now, let's explore how AI can transform your social media strategy, simplifying content creation and scheduling without sacrificing quality or authenticity.

Managing social media demands both time and creativity. With AI, creating and curating content no longer needs to be a resource-intensive process. AI tools can help you quickly generate posts, captions, hashtags, and even visuals that are tailored to your brand, helping you stay consistent and relevant with minimal effort.

Automating Social Media Posts with AI Tools

One of the biggest challenges in social media management is creating consistent, on-brand posts. Fortunately, AI tools can handle everything from drafting captions to scheduling posts. For example, platforms like **Jasper.ai** enable you to generate tailored captions simply by entering a few details about your topic, audience, or style. Jasper can then produce polished captions that resonate with your followers.

This streamlined approach makes it easy to plan a week's worth of posts, helping you stay consistent without spending hours brainstorming and drafting each post individually. By automating the content creation process, you save valuable time and ensure that your messaging aligns smoothly across all posts.

Creating Engaging Content that Resonates

Success on social media is about more than just frequent posting—it's also about building genuine connections with your audience. AI tools help by analyzing what types of posts have engaged your followers in the past and by crafting content designed to replicate that success. Tools like **Lately.ai,** for instance, can analyze the style and tone of your most popular posts and generate similar content, increasing your likelihood of engaging with your audience, which is your ultimate goal.

AI can also help you tailor content to specific platforms. For instance, Twitter posts need to be concise and compelling, while LinkedIn allows for more in-depth, professional messaging. AI ensures that your content is optimized for each platform's unique format, helping you create a unified and effective social media presence.

Balancing Automation with Authenticity

While AI can streamline much of the content creation process and provide insights into what resonates with your audience, it's important not solely to rely on automation. Social media followers value genuine interactions and can quickly recognize when content feels impersonal or overly automated. Strive to balance AI-driven efficiency with personal engagement by setting aside time to respond to comments, share updates, and interact directly with your followers. This approach helps build a social media presence that feels engaging, approachable, and true to your brand's voice.

Note of Caution: AI is a valuable tool for efficiency and consistency, but over-reliance on automation can dilute the personal connection that makes social media effective. Always review and personalize AI-generated content to ensure it aligns with your brand's unique tone and values.

AI-Powered Tools for Social Media Content Creation

Here are a few standout AI tools for social media management that can help you create, optimize, and schedule posts effortlessly:

- **Buffer and Hootsuite**: Both platforms now integrate AI to help you create, schedule, and optimize posts for engagement across multiple platforms simultaneously, allowing you to streamline your entire social media process.
- **Canva**: A versatile design platform with AI features and ready-to-use templates to create, customize, and plan stunning visuals, simplifying social media management.
- **DALL-E:** For visuals, DALL-E offers a user-friendly way to create custom images. Just type a prompt that describes your desired image, and DALL-E will generate visuals that align with your brand's aesthetic.
- **Jasper.ai**: Known for its ability to create high-quality content, Jasper.ai helps you generate tailored social media posts based on your desired tone, audience, and message. You simply input a prompt, and the AI suggests relevant text to post.
- **Lately.ai**: Lately.ai analyzes your past social media performance to generate content that resonates with your audience. Understanding what has worked well in the past, Lately.ai will create new posts that have a higher likelihood of engaging your followers.

These tools can help you write captions, generate relevant hashtags, and even craft engaging content for specific platforms like Instagram, Twitter, LinkedIn, and Facebook—all without having to start from scratch.

Hands-On Exercise: Crafting a Week's Worth of Social Media Content

Complexity Rating: 2/5

Estimated Time: 20–30 minutes for initial setup; about 5 minutes per day to review and refine

For this exercise, we'll use **Jasper.ai** and **DALL-E** to create a week's worth of social media posts, complete with images and captions. This streamlined process ensures you're ready with engaging, on-brand content for the entire week:

1. **Choose Your Theme or Product:** Select a theme for your posts, such as promoting a product, service, or upcoming event. For example, let's say you're promoting a "natural wellness brand."
2. **Generate Captions with Jasper.ai:** Open Jasper.ai and enter a clear prompt to create captions. For instance, try: *"Generate seven Instagram captions for a natural wellness brand, focusing on eco-friendly ingredients and health benefits."*
    - Jasper will provide multiple caption options. Review each one and make any necessary adjustments to ensure they fit your brand's voice.
3. **Create Visuals with DALL-E:** For each caption, think of an image concept that complements the message. Open DALL-E and enter prompts that align with each caption. For example:
    - *"A close-up of wellness products surrounded by fresh green leaves and soft lighting"*
    - *"A minimalistic bathroom setting with wellness products and a clean, calming vibe"*
        - DALL-E will generate visuals that you can download and use for your posts.
4. **Organize and Schedule Your Posts:** Using a scheduling tool like **Buffer** or **Hootsuite**, upload each caption with its corresponding image. These tools can recommend optimal

posting times based on engagement patterns to maximize visibility.

5. **Review and Refine Daily:** Each day, take a few minutes to engage with any comments or messages on your posts. This keeps your presence authentic while letting AI handle the bulk of content creation.

Follow these steps and you'll have an entire week's worth of social media content ready to go—generated, optimized, and scheduled–in less time than it would typically take to create a single post. This not only boosts your productivity but also removes the guesswork from content creation so you can focus on growing your online presence.

Best Practices for Using AI on Social Media

While AI can handle much of the content creation process, here are a few best practices to maximize its effectiveness:

- **Be Clear and Specific**: The more detailed your prompts, the better the AI-generated content will align with your goals.
- **Review for Authenticity**: Before publishing, check the content to ensure it feels authentic and represents your brand's voice.
- **Balance Automation with Engagement**: Use AI to streamline posts but dedicate time for 1:1 interactions with your audience.
- **Stay Flexible**: Experiment with different prompts and content formats to discover what works best for your audience.

Key Takeaways:

- **AI streamlines social media management**: Tools like **Jasper.ai** and **DALL-E** help you quickly create high-quality posts and maintain a consistent online presence.
- **AI enhances engagement through data analysis**: By learning from past performance, AI tools like **Lately.ai** help

you create posts that are more likely to engage your audience.

- **Scheduling tools boost consistency**: Platforms like **Buffer** and **Hootsuite** make it easy to organize and schedule your AI-generated content, freeing you to focus on growth and strategy.

4.4 HOW AI IMPROVES THE CUSTOMER EXPERIENCE

Now that we've examined how AI can enhance marketing strategies, let's shift focus to another essential aspect: customer experience. Beyond just reaching customers, AI transforms how businesses connect with and support them. AI tools allow companies to provide smoother, more personalized, and proactive experiences that feel intuitive to customers. In this section, we'll look at how AI can improve customer support through responsive **chatbots**, tailor experiences with precise recommendations, analyze customer feedback, and even anticipate customer needs—helping you build deeper connections that keep customers coming back.

AI-Powered Customer Support

AI-driven customer support has come a long way in the past few years, significantly improving how businesses respond to and resolve customer queries. Gone are the days when chatbots could only answer basic, scripted questions. Today's AI-powered support systems are much more advanced and capable of handling complex inquiries. These tools can provide instant, accurate answers while simulating human-like conversation, making the entire process more natural and seamless for customers.

One of the leading benefits of using AI in customer service is resolving issues faster and, yes, even more efficiently. AI systems can quickly analyze customer questions, identify relevant information, and provide accurate answers or solutions—all within seconds. This instant response reduces wait times and eliminates the need for customers to navigate through frustrating phone menus or long email chains. Whether it's a chatbot resolving basic inquiries or an AI-driven ticketing system routing more complex issues to human agents, AI ensures that customers receive timely support.

Additionally, AI's continuous learning capabilities enable systems to improve over time. AI can offer increasingly relevant responses by analyzing past interactions, further enhancing customer experiences. The more a business relies on AI for customer service, the better and more accurate the system becomes. Like humans, AI learns and becomes more intelligent with repetition and time.

For customers, this results in a smoother, more efficient support experience. Instead of waiting in long queues or searching for the answers themselves, they get quick, reliable assistance at any time of day or night. For businesses, this leads to increased customer satisfaction, lower operational costs, and a more efficient support process.

Analyzing Customer Feedback with AI

One of the best ways to improve customer satisfaction is by actively listening to feedback, and AI makes this process far more efficient and insightful.

AI-powered tools for **sentiment analysis** help businesses understand customer emotions and opinions across various sources—such as online reviews, social media posts, and surveys. These tools can identify positive, neutral, and negative sentiments, offering a broad view of how customers feel about your products or services.

AI also simplifies feedback aggregation. Pulling insights from multiple platforms into a single, digestible format makes it easier to identify trends, spot recurring issues, and act on them. For instance, if AI detects customers frequently mentioning long wait times in reviews, this feedback can be swiftly addressed, improving operations and customer satisfaction.

AI-powered feedback analysis helps businesses respond quickly to issues before they grow. Whether adjusting product features, speeding up response times, or fixing service gaps, AI provides companies with the insights needed to keep customers happy. This proactive approach shows customers that their feedback matters, building loyalty and trust.

Proactive Customer Engagement

Listening to feedback is essential for customer satisfaction, but what if you could solve a customer issue *before* it arises? AI makes this possible through **proactive engagement**, one of its mighty innovations in enhancing customer experience. By analyzing customer behavior in the moment, AI can anticipate needs and offer timely solutions, often before a customer even reaches out for help.

For example, suppose AI detects that a customer has been browsing your website for an extended period without making a purchase. In that case, a chatbot can proactively step in to offer assistance or recommend products to guide them toward completing their transaction. This proactive engagement helps prevent frustration and streamlines the customer's journey, creating a smoother, more efficient experience.

AI tools can also send personalized notifications based on customer preferences, previous purchases, or interactions. Imagine receiving a reminder to reorder a product you previously bought or a personalized discount on an item you browsed a few days ago. These interactions aren't just convenient—they also increase customer engagement and loyalty.

Anticipating needs before they arise and delivering relevant offers at the right time helps businesses build stronger customer connections, leading to greater satisfaction and lasting loyalty.

Tools for AI-Driven Customer Experience

These tools help businesses engage with and support customers more effectively by streamlining interactions, tailoring experiences, and addressing needs proactively. They also simplify customer support and make gathering and analyzing feedback more accessible:

- **Grammarly:** While primarily a writing tool, Grammarly ensures that customer communications via chat or email are polished and professional.
- **Landbot**: An intuitive no-code chatbot platform that helps businesses create interactive, personalized conversational experiences for customer feedback, support, and engagement, all without requiring technical expertise.
- **ManyChat:** A user-friendly platform for building chatbots to automate customer interactions, commonly used on websites and Facebook Messenger to engage visitors in real-time.

Hands-On Exercise: Setting Up a Customer Feedback Chatbot on Landbot

Complexity Rating: 3/5

Estimated Time: 30

In this exercise, we'll set up a pre-built **Customer Feedback** chatbot on **Landbot** and make a few simple customizations to show you how user-friendly and intuitive this platform is. The goal is to create a functional chatbot that collects valuable feedback while learning how to personalize it to reflect your unique style.

1. **Sign Up and Choose Your Starting Template** Visit **Landbot** and create a free account. Follow the onboarding steps to get familiar with the platform. Once you're on the dashboard, click **Build a Chatbot** and select **Web** as your bot type. From the available templates, choose **Customer Feedback.**
    - *(Note: Landbot's options may change over time. If this exact template isn't available, pick one that seems close to your needs—don't stress about perfection, just get started!)*
2. **Preview and Test the Template:** Once you select your prebuilt template, click **Test this Bot** to see the default chatbot in action. Familiarize yourself with the flow and think

about where you might want to make small changes, such as rephrasing questions or adding extra steps to personalize it.

3. **Add a Question to Ask for Their Name:** To make your chatbot more engaging, add a question that asks for the user's name and uses it in the next message:
   - After the first greeting block in the flow, click the + to the right of the block to add a new block.
   - Select **Questions**, then choose **Ask for a name**.
   - Personalize the block further by editing the default question.
     - Default: "What's your name?"
     - Updated: "Hi there! We'd love to get to know you. What's your name?"
4. **Address Them by Their Name:** Once you've added the **Name Question** block, add a + to connect it to the next prebuilt question. Update the text in the next question to include their name dynamically. For example:
   - *"Hi [Name]! Great to meet you!"*
     - To insert the user's name, use Landbot's built-in variable feature (e.g., @name). This makes the chatbot feel more personalized and engaging.
5. **Add More Feedback Questions:** Include additional questions to encourage thoughtful responses or make the conversation more interactive. For example:
   - Open-Ended Question: *"What did you enjoy most about your experience?"*
   - Ask for a **Rating** with Emojis: *"Rate us! ⭐⭐⭐⭐⭐"*
6. **Optional–Ask For a Google Review**: If users give a five-star ⭐⭐⭐⭐⭐ rating, take it a step further by asking them to leave a review for you. Make it easy by providing a direct link to your Google Review page.
7. **Experiment, Test, and Publish:** Don't stop here! Experiment with features like adding follow-up questions, using conditional logic to create unique responses, or even inserting fun GIFs to surprise users.

- Try out your new flow by clicking **Test this Bot** to see how users will experience it. Once you're satisfied with the chatbot, click **Publish** to make it live. You'll receive a shareable link or embed code to place it on your website or share with your audience.

In just eight simple steps, you've built and customized a chatbot that collects customer feedback. This exercise demonstrates how easy Landbot is to use and encourages you to explore its features to get creative with your chatbot's personality and functionality. Even if you're not running a business, your friendly AI-powered chatbot can make any blog, portfolio, or personal website feel more interactive and engaging.

Best Practices for AI-Driven Customer Experience

Here are a few best practices to help you get the most out of AI-powered customer experience tools:

- **Balance AI with Human Touch**: While AI can handle routine tasks, you should always maintain a human element for more complex or sensitive customer issues. This balance ensures a positive, personalized customer experience.
- **Personalize Interactions**: Use AI to gather data and personalize customer interactions. Tailored recommendations, special offers, and proactive engagement increase loyalty and make customers feel valued.
- **Continuously Improve with Feedback**: Use AI tools for sentiment analysis and feedback aggregation to continually improve your services. The more you listen to your customers, the better you can meet their needs.

Key Takeaways:

- **AI enhances customer support**: AI **chatbots** handle common queries efficiently, ensuring faster response times and improving overall customer satisfaction.

- **AI personalizes the customer experience**: By analyzing data, AI delivers tailored recommendations and personalized marketing campaigns, making customers feel valued.
- **AI helps businesses stay proactive**: Predictive analytics and proactive engagement tools allow you to anticipate customer needs, offering timely solutions and enhancing the overall customer journey.

You are now equipped to leverage AI to enhance customer experiences, strengthen client relationships, boost satisfaction levels, and keep your business ahead of your competition.

4.5 BRAINSTORMING BUSINESS IDEAS WITH AI MAGIC

We've already seen how generative AI can assist with professional tasks like writing, editing, and content creation. Let's take things a step further and explore how AI can be a game-changer when brainstorming and refining business ideas. Whether you're looking to start a new business or grow an existing one, AI can offer fresh perspectives and valuable insights driven by market trends and consumer behavior.

In this chapter, we'll explore how tools like **ChatGPT** and **IdeaBuddy** can take you beyond generating ideas to developing comprehensive business plans. For example, ChatGPT can brainstorm creative concepts, while IdeaBuddy helps structure those ideas into actionable plans.

Generating Innovative Ideas

AI can leverage data and trends to suggest business ideas tailored to market demands. For instance, a prompt like:

"Generate business ideas in the wellness sector that focus on sustainability and personalized solutions" might yield responses such as:

- An eco-friendly subscription box for sustainable health products

- Personalized wellness coaching apps that track individual progress and offer customized advice
- A fitness platform that rewards users for sustainable lifestyle changes, integrating environmental impact reduction as part of its goals

These suggestions are not only creative but are relevant to market demands. With AI's ability to analyze trends instantly, you can discover business ideas that inspire you and are practical steps toward your next venture.

Building a Business Plan

Once you've settled on your business idea, IdeaBuddy helps you turn that concept into a fully structured business plan. The tool guides you through essential steps like market analysis, revenue modeling, and competitor insights. For example, if you choose the personalized wellness app idea, IdeaBuddy can help you outline everything from your target audience to growth strategies.

It also simplifies business validation by offering templates for creating a business model canvas, financial projections, and strategic plans. You'll be guided through questions such as:

- Who is your target market?
- What is your value proposition?
- What are your costs and projected revenues?

By breaking down complex business planning into manageable steps, IdeaBuddy helps you move quickly from idea to execution without feeling overwhelmed. Whether you're building a new plan or refining an existing one, this tool makes the process straightforward and systematic.

Evaluating and Refining Your Ideas

Once you've developed your business idea and mapped out your plan, refining it with AI-powered market analysis tools can strengthen its feasibility. Tools like **Exploding Topics** help you evaluate the market and identify gaps by offering insights into competitors, customer demand, and potential risks.

For example, if you're considering launching a personalized wellness app, you can use Exploding Topics to assess the market landscape. This competitive analysis helps refine your idea, ensuring it meets market needs. Important questions to consider might include:

- What wellness trends are gaining traction among consumers?
- Who are the leading competitors?
- What unique features will set your app apart?

It's also important to evaluate risks. AI tools can forecast potential challenges that could impact your success, like market shifts or evolving customer preferences. By providing a comprehensive view of both opportunities and risks, AI ensures your business idea is not only innovative but also viable.

Tools for Brainstorming Business Ideas with AI

These tools will help you generate, evaluate, and refine business ideas using AI. They offer insights into market trends, customer behavior, and competitor strategies, making the business planning process more data-driven and effective:

- **ChatGPT**: A versatile AI tool that generates creative business ideas based on input prompts. It helps brainstorm innovative ideas in various industries, including wellness, tech, and sustainability.
- **Exploding Topics**: A platform that uses AI to identify emerging trends across industries, helping you validate business ideas by providing insights into growing markets and consumer interests.
- **IdeaBuddy**: A business planning platform that guides users through structuring their ideas into comprehensive business

plans. It offers templates for business model canvases, financial plans, and market analysis, helping you validate and refine your ideas.

Hands-On Exercise: Using AI to Brainstorm and Refine a Business Idea

Complexity Rating: 3/5

Estimated Time: 30-45 minutes

Explore how AI tools can help you brainstorm, structure, and refine a business idea. In this exercise, we'll use **ChatGPT** to generate ideas, **IdeaBuddy** to structure your concept, and **Exploding Topics** to identify emerging trends. Follow these steps to see how AI simplifies the process of turning a concept into a market-ready plan.

1. **Generate Ideas with ChatGPT**: Open **ChatGPT** and ask for innovative ideas. Use a prompt like: *"Generate innovative business ideas for a wellness startup focused on sustainability."*
    - Review the AI suggestions and select one that resonates with your interests or goals. Don't be afraid to tweak or combine ideas to align with your vision.
2. **Structure Your Idea with IdeaBuddy**: Visit **IdeaBuddy** and select the **Business Guide** template to organize your chosen idea. Fill in key sections such as:
    - **Concept:** Briefly describe your idea and its purpose.
    - **Research:** Highlight potential markets and customer needs.
    - **Set Up:** Outline how the business will operate.
    - **Projections:** Create an initial financial overview.
    - If you get stuck, use the **AI Buddy** feature within IdeaBuddy for suggestions and guidance. This tool will walk you through creating a solid business model.
3. **Conduct Market Research with Exploding Topics**: Use **Exploding Topics** to uncover emerging trends related to

your business idea. Enter relevant keywords like *"sustainable wellness"* or *"personalized fitness"* to explore new consumer interests and untapped opportunities. Use this information to identify how your idea can align with or capitalize on these trends.

   - *(Note: Advanced trend searches are available with the paid Pro version, but general topic searches can be explored for free.)*

4. **Map Out the Competition:** Shift focus to your competitors. Search for businesses in your chosen industry and analyze their:
   - Key offerings and strengths
   - Market positioning and customer reach
   - Areas where their offerings fall short
     - Use this analysis to spot gaps in the market that your business could fill or ways to differentiate your product or service.
5. **Refine Your Business Idea**: Based on the data from Exploding Topics refine your original idea. You might tweak your product offering, adjust your target market, or incorporate new features. Continue to iterate until you've developed a solid, market-ready concept.

By the end of this exercise, you'll have a viable business idea and a structured plan backed by data that is refined with AI insights. This hands-on approach demonstrates how AI tools can simplify the journey from concept to execution, empowering you to create innovative and competitive business models.

Best Practices for Using AI in Business Brainstorming

To get the most out of AI tools during brainstorming:

- **Use Data to Inform Creativity**: Don't just rely on creative inspiration—use AI to back up your ideas with data on market trends and competitor behavior.
- **Start Broad, Then Narrow**: Begin with general prompts

and refine your ideas, as AI tools offer more specific data and insights.

- **Iterate and Refine**: Business planning is an iterative process. Use AI to continually refine your idea based on new data and market shifts.

Key Takeaways:

- **AI enhances business idea generation**: **ChatGPT** and **IdeaBuddy** help you brainstorm creative ideas based on real-time market data and trends.
- **AI structures and refines your ideas**: **IdeaBuddy** guides you from concept to execution by helping you create business models and financial plans.
- **AI provides critical insights for evaluation**: **Exploding Topics** offers competitor analysis and market research, helping you refine your business idea and assess its feasibility.

YOUR WORDS CAN HELP SOMEONE TAKE THEIR FIRST STEP

"*When you learn, teach. When you get, give.*"

— *MAYA ANGELOU*

Did you know that sharing something as simple as your experience can create a ripple effect for others?

Think about someone just like you—curious about AI, excited to learn, but maybe a little unsure about where to start. Your review could be the encouragement they need to take that first step with confidence.

My mission with *AI Mastery for Beginners* is to make learning about AI **simple, approachable, and stress-free** for anyone ready to explore. But to help more people discover the power of AI, **I need your voice.**

Most readers rely on reviews to decide if a book is worth their time. That means *your words matter*.

If you feel this book earned a **5-star review**, I'd be so grateful if you'd take a moment to share your thoughts.

Leaving a review is **free**, takes **less than a minute**, and could inspire someone to start their AI journey. Your review could inspire:

- A busy professional reclaiming hours in their week.
- An ambitious entrepreneur streamlining tasks to focus on growth.
- A busy parent simplifying daily life with AI.
- A lifelong learner unlocking AI's potential for new possibilities.
- A curious beginner building confidence with creative tools.

Ready to make a difference? Scan the QR code below to leave your review.

If you love empowering others, you're my kind of person.

Thank you so much for being part of this journey and for helping share the magic of AI with the world!

Yours in curiosity and growth,
Maura Vella

5

AI IN PERSONAL LIFE

So far, we've explored how AI can accelerate professional growth and productivity. Now, we'll focus on the ways it can impact your personal life. AI isn't just revolutionizing the workplace—it's becoming a powerful tool for health, organization, and leisure, making daily tasks smoother and more enjoyable.

5.1 AI FOR WELLNESS: FITNESS, NUTRITION, HEALTH MONITORING, AND STRESS REDUCTION

Taking care of your health is at the core of living a fulfilling, enjoyable life, and AI-powered tools are making it easier than ever. These innovative systems create personalized fitness plans, monitor your activity, and guide your nutrition choices, providing you with insights to optimize your health and feel your best. Whether you're refining a workout, tracking health metrics, or optimizing your diet, AI offers a range of solutions that make achieving your wellness goals effortless, freeing you to focus on living your best life.

AI-Generated Fitness Plans

Before AI, maintaining a consistent and effective fitness routine often meant relying on the guidance of a personal trainer. Today, AI is transforming how we approach exercise, making it easier and more accessible to everyone. Apps like **Peloton Guide**, **JRNY**, and **Fitbod** offer personalized workout plans designed to match your fitness level, goals, and preferences—all without the need for constant guidance from a trainer. These tools can even complement a trainer's expertise, providing additional data and insights to enhance personalized training sessions.

These AI-driven tools start by collecting your personal information, such as age, weight, fitness goals, and preferred workout styles. For example, if your focus is building muscle, the app will create a strength-based regimen with specific exercises and recommended weights. If you're aiming for cardiovascular health, the AI might suggest a mix of running, cycling, and HIIT workouts.

What sets these fitness tools apart from traditional workout plans is their adaptability. As you progress, the AI tracks your performance, modifying the intensity and difficulty of your workouts in the moment. Whether you require a lighter session after a poor night's sleep or a more challenging routine as you get stronger, AI ensures your plan evolves with your needs. This personalized approach keeps your workouts effective and fresh, helps prevent burnout and injury, and promotes the long-term success of your fitness journey.

Nutrition and Diet Planning Made Simple with AI

Good nutrition is essential for overall wellness, but meal planning is often time-consuming and monotonous. AI-powered apps like **MyFitnessPal**, **Lumen**, and **Viome** simplify this process by analyzing your dietary needs and preferences to provide personalized guidance.

These tools cater to specific goals and preferences—whether vegan, keto, or gluten-free—by tracking calories, macronutrients, and other key metrics. For instance, if weight loss is your goal, AI can suggest meals that support a caloric deficit while ensuring balanced nutrition.

Some apps, like Viome, even use advanced data, such as gut microbiome analysis, to refine recommendations tailored to your unique biology.

As you log meals, the AI evolves its suggestions, ensuring your nutrition plan stays aligned with your progress and goals.

Health Monitoring with AI: Be Your Own Wellness Coach

Staying on top of your overall health is essential for achieving fitness and wellness goals, and AI-powered devices like **Fitbit**, **Oura Ring**, and **Whoop Strap** make it easier than ever. These wearables go beyond tracking basic metrics—they analyze your heart rate, sleep quality, activity levels, and recovery to provide a complete picture of your physical well-being.

For example, Oura tracks sleep cycles and heart rate variability (HRV), delivering personalized insights to help you optimize recovery and daily energy levels. Whoop specializes in monitoring strain and recovery, offering tailored recommendations to prevent overtraining and support sustainable progress. Fitbit, a versatile and widely accessible option, tracks steps, calories burned, and even stress levels, making it a great entry point for fitness and health monitoring.

These devices also integrate seamlessly with other AI tools, helping you connect the dots between your activity, nutrition, and recovery. For instance, after Oura detects a night of poor sleep, you might use the insights to adjust your exercise intensity for the day. This data-driven approach empowers you to take charge of your health and make informed decisions that align with your goals.

By leveraging these advanced AI-powered tools, you can transform raw health data into actionable insights, keeping your wellness journey on track with precision and ease.

Stress Reduction and Mindfulness

Managing stress and supporting mental well-being are essential for overall health. Innovative tools like **Headspace**, **Muse**, and **Calm** make it easier than ever to manage stress and practice mindfulness.

These apps and wearables offer personalized insights and techniques to help you relax, focus, and build a sustainable mindfulness routine.

Headspace uses AI to create personalized programs for stress relief, relaxation, and improved focus, gently adapting its recommendations as you progress toward your goals. The Muse wearable enhances your meditation practice by using advanced sensors to monitor brain activity, providing real-time feedback that helps you stay focused and find more profound calm. Meanwhile, Calm offers soothing guided meditations, breathing exercises, and sleep stories designed to ease anxiety and bring clarity to your mind. By using machine learning to adapt to your unique preferences and habits, Calm helps you effortlessly find moments of peace in your day.

These tools increase awareness of mindfulness's benefits and make it more accessible with customizable solutions that seamlessly fit into daily life. Whether you're refining your meditation practice with Muse, learning mindfulness techniques with Headspace, or relaxing with Calm, these tools empower you to manage stress effectively and prioritize mental wellness.

AI-Powered Wellness Apps and Wearables to Check Out

Here are just a handful of AI-powered wellness apps and wearables that are revolutionizing health management by offering personalized insights and syncing data across platforms for a complete view of your physical and mental well-being:

Apple Health: A comprehensive app that tracks various health metrics, including activity.

Calm: App geared toward improving sleep and reducing stress with guided meditation, sleep stories, and relaxation techniques.

Fitbit: Tracks steps, heart rate, and other fitness metrics, syncing with other apps to provide a complete picture of your physical activity.

Fitbod: A personalized fitness app that uses AI to generate tailored workout routines based on your strength training goals, available equipment, and progress.

Google Fit: Tracks your activity, heart rate, and fitness progress while syncing with other health apps and devices.

Headspace: AI-powered mindfulness and meditation app that offers personalized recommendations for reducing stress and improving mental health.

JRNY: An AI-powered fitness app that generates personalized workout routines and adapts them based on your progress.

Lifesum: Helps you eat healthier by offering personalized meal plans and food tracking to reach your goals.

Lumen: A personalized nutrition app that measures metabolism and provides tailored meal suggestions to help users achieve their health goals.

MyFitnessPal: AI app for tracking food intake, calories, and macronutrients, syncing with fitness trackers for an integrated health overview.

Muse: A wearable device that uses AI to monitor brain activity and provide real-time feedback during meditation, helping users improve focus, relaxation, and mindfulness.

Noom: Uses psychology and AI to help you make healthier food choices and build long-term habits.

Oura: Advanced wearable ring that monitors sleep, activity, and recovery to provide holistic insights into health.

Peloton Guide: Offers personalized workout recommendations based on your fitness goals and data.

Sleep Cycle: Analyzes individual sleep patterns and wakes you up at the optimal time, leaving you feeling more rested.

Tempo Studio: Provides real-time feedback on your form during workouts using a smart mirror, helping to prevent injury and optimize performance.

Viome: An AI-driven platform that analyzes gut microbiome data to provide personalized dietary and supplement recommendations.

Whoop Strap: An advanced fitness tracker that monitors sleep, recovery, and strain, offering insights into optimizing workouts and recovery times.

Hands-On Exercise: Setting Small, Achievable Wellness Goals with AI Support

Complexity Rating: 1/5

Estimated Time: 15-20 minutes

This exercise is designed for anyone who feels overwhelmed by the idea of starting a new fitness or nutrition plan. Instead of diving into a big commitment, you'll use any AI-powered app to set one small, manageable goal that you can easily integrate into your daily routine. The aim is to build momentum, focus on progress, and create a positive association with your wellness journey.

1. **Choose One Focus Area:** Take a moment to reflect on your current lifestyle and decide on one small, achievable focus area. Choose something that feels most realistic and motivating for you right now. For example:
   - Fitness: Adding 10 minutes of movement to your day
   - Nutrition: Tracking just one meal per day
   - Mental Wellness: Practicing 5 minutes of mindfulness or relaxation
     - This focus area will guide the type of app you choose in the next step.

2. **Select an AI-Powered App:** Choose an app that matches your focus area, or use one you discover on your own.
   - Fitness: Fitbit, JRNY, Google Fit, Fitbod, Peloton Guide, Tempo Studio
   - Nutrition: MyFitnessPal, Lifesum, Lumen, Viome, Noom
   - Mental Wellness: Calm, Headspace, Muse, Sleep Cycle
   - General Health Monitoring: Apple Health, Oura, Whoop Strap
     - For example, try **Fitbod** for workout plans, **MyFitnessPal** for tracking meals, or **Headspace** for quick mindfulness exercises. Select the app that feels most relevant and manageable for your goal.
3. **Set a Small, Daily Goal in the App:** Use the app's tools to create a tiny, manageable goal.
   - Fitness: Set a daily step target (e.g., 5,000 steps instead of 10,000)
   - Nutrition: Log one meal or snack per day instead of everything
   - Mental Wellness: Schedule a 5-minute guided meditation or breathing exercise
4. **Schedule a Reminder:** Use the app's notification feature, your AI virtual assistant, or your phone's calendar to schedule a reminder for your new habit. For example, set up a 7:30 a.m. notification to track your breakfast or a 6:00 p.m. alert for a short walk. Have fun–make your reminder encouraging you to keep yourself motivated and say something like, *"You're doing great—log your breakfast now!"*
5. **Take One Action Today:** Complete your small goal for the day using the app. Focus only on today's action and celebrate completing it, no matter how small it feels.
   - Log one meal
   - Take a 10-minute walk
   - Do a short guided meditation
6. **Reflect and Adjust:** After completing your goal for a few days, reflect on how it feels. Is it manageable? Are you noticing small wins, like more energy or focus? Adjust your

goal if needed. If it feels too hard, scale it back. If it feels easy, take one small step forward, like tracking two meals instead of one.

7. **Celebrate Your Consistency:** At the end of the week, take time to celebrate your progress. Even small, consistent efforts deserve recognition! Here are some ways to celebrate:
   - Acknowledge your effort: Review your app's tracking features (e.g., your steps graph in Fitbit, or logged meals in MyFitnessPal) to see how far you've come.
   - Share your success: If you feel comfortable, tell a friend or family member about your progress or post about it.
   - Treat yourself: Reward yourself with something uplifting—a relaxing activity, a favorite healthy snack, or a small indulgence like a new playlist or fitness gear.

Shift the focus from big, overwhelming goals to manageable, daily actions. Let AI tools guide and support you to help you gain confidence, build momentum, and establish a sustainable approach to wellness. Remember, we're not aiming for perfection; we're looking for progress, one small step at a time.

Key Takeaways:

- **AI creates personalized fitness and nutrition plans**: Apps like **Fitbod** and **MyFitnessPal** tailor workouts and meals to your goals, adapting as you progress to keep you motivated and on track.
- **Health monitoring becomes actionable with AI**: Wearables like **Fitbit** and **Oura** track sleep, activity, and recovery, providing insights to help you make smarter decisions about your well-being.
- **AI makes mindfulness more accessible**: Tools like **Calm** and **Headspace** offer guided relaxation and stress management techniques personalized to your preferences and habits.

5.2 LET AI BE YOUR PERSONAL SHOPPER

With your wellness routine in place, let's use AI to make your life easier in other areas, too. Ready to simplify your shopping? Let's explore how AI can be your personal assistant, find the best deals, curate items based on your style, and save you time and energy.

Shopping has never been more convenient, thanks to the integration of AI into the retail world. Whether you're looking for the best deals, personalized recommendations, or even assistance with grocery shopping, AI offers a level of convenience and customization that takes the hassle out of everyday tasks.

AI for Personalized Shopping Recommendations

AI is revolutionizing the way we shop by analyzing habits, preferences, and browsing history to create a faster, simpler, and more tailored experience. Rather than feeling intrusive, these tools are designed to save you time and effort, helping you find what you need with ease.

For example, Amazon's **Rufus**, an AI-powered assistant in the Amazon Shopping app, provides real-time product suggestions and answers questions based on your browsing habits and past purchases. Over time, Rufus learns your preferences and refines its recommendations, aligning with your unique style and shopping goals.

Similarly, Google's AI-enhanced Shopping tab leverages your search history and sophisticated algorithms to surface products that match your interests, whether you're looking for everyday essentials or special gifts. These tools work quietly in the background to create an intuitive shopping experience and offer interactive features when you need them.

By adapting to your preferences over time, AI transforms shopping into a personalized, efficient, and stress-free journey, helping you discover products you'll love without endless searching.

Tracking Prices and Finding Deals

Gone are the days of endlessly searching for the best prices. AI-powered apps like **Honey** and **ShopSavvy** scan the internet for coupons and track price drops to ensure you get the best deal possible. These tools take the guesswork out of bargain hunting and allow you to shop with confidence, knowing you've found the lowest price.

With apps like **Google Shopping**, AI will even compare prices across different retailers and notify you when prices drop so you can purchase at the most optimal time. For frequent travelers, tools like **Hopper**—which we touched on in Chapter 2— provide similar benefits, such as tracking flight and hotel prices to help you book when prices are at their lowest.

Tools for AI-Powered Shopping Assistance

These tools can help you get personalized shopping recommendations, track price changes, and find the best deals with minimal effort, saving you time and money:

- **Google Shopping**: An AI-powered tool that compares prices from different retailers and helps you track price changes to purchase items at the lowest possible cost.
- **Honey**: A browser extension that automatically searches for and applies the best coupons available when you shop online, helping you save on purchases across various retailers.
- **Hopper:** Predicts flight and hotel price fluctuations and notifies you of the best time to book.
- **ShopSavvy**: An app that tracks prices across multiple retailers and notifies you when prices drop, allowing you to get the best deal on products.

These AI-powered tools take the stress out of shopping, offering personalized recommendations and ensuring users get the best deals possible, all while saving time and effort.

Now, let's explore how you can use AI to become a smarter shopper and find the best deals with minimal effort.

Hands-On Exercise: Using AI to Find the Best Shopping Deals

Complexity Rating: 2/5

Estimated Time: 15-20 minutes

1. **Download an AI Shopping Assistant**: Download a shopping assistant like **Honey**, **ShopSavvy**, or **Google Shopping**.
2. **Set Up Price Alerts**: Choose a product you're interested in purchasing, such as a new laptop or pair of shoes. Set up a price alert on your app of choice so you'll be notified when the price drops or coupons become available.
3. **Search for Coupons or Deals**: Use Honey to search for active coupons across various online stores. Simply browse your favorite retailer's website, and Honey will automatically apply the best coupons available at checkout.
4. **Track Price Trends**: Use ShopSavvy or Google Shopping to track price trends on the product you're interested in. Monitor how the price fluctuates over a week or two and decide when the best time to buy is.
5. **Review the Savings**: Once you make a purchase, review the discounts you've applied and see how much AI helped you save. Reflect on how these tools made the shopping experience easier and more cost-effective.

By the end of this exercise, you'll be equipped to shop smarter and faster with the help of AI, saving both time and money in the process.

Key Takeaways:

- **AI tools help personalize your shopping experience**: By learning your preferences, AI shopping assistants can suggest products that match your style and needs.
- **AI makes it easier to find deals**: Whether it's price tracking or automatically applying coupons, AI ensures you're getting the best possible price.
- **Using multiple AI tools together enhances your savings**: By combining different AI-driven apps, you can track deals, set price alerts, and apply coupons all at the same time.

5.3 LEARNING NEW HOBBIES WITH A LITTLE HELP FROM AI

Starting a new hobby can feel overwhelming, but AI simplifies the process, allowing you to learn new skills comfortably at your own pace. Whether you want to explore photography, cooking, painting, or even mastering a musical instrument, AI tools can act as personal guides, offering step-by-step instructions, personalized feedback, and curated content based on your progress. With AI as your teacher, you can explore new hobbies with confidence and ease.

AI for Skill Development

One of the most innovative and distinctive ways AI can help you pick up a new hobby, compared to traditional methods, is by personalizing the learning experience. Tools like **Skillshare**, **YouTube**, and **MasterClass** use AI algorithms to recommend courses, tutorials, and videos that match your interests and skill level. Whether you're just beginning or want to deepen an existing passion, AI ensures you get the most relevant and engaging content.

Personalized Recommendations for Skill Progression

AI tools don't just teach—they grow with you. By tracking your progress, these tools adapt to your evolving skill level, keeping you motivated while avoiding burnout. For example, if learning a new language is on your list, apps like **Duolingo** use AI to create adaptive lesson plans tailored to your progress, ensuring you build your skills at a comfortable pace. If you're learning to play a musical instrument, platforms like **Yousician** offer real-time feedback and adjust exercises based on your performance, helping you refine your technique and improve with every session.

SideChef is a powerful example of how AI can adapt to your needs, whether you're just starting to cook or you're a seasoned pro looking to streamline your routine. The app tailors meal suggestions and recipes to your skill level and preferences, providing step-by-step guidance for beginners and more advanced options for experienced cooks. SideChef also simplifies grocery shopping by creating shoppable lists and connecting you with delivery services, helping you save time and focus on refining your culinary skills. This adaptive approach ensures your cooking experience is both efficient and rewarding, no matter your experience level.

Adaptive learning creates a tailored experience, ensuring that you always stay motivated and challenged but never overwhelmed. AI can guide you through a learning journey that evolves with your progress, offering the right balance of challenge and encouragement to keep you inspired.

Tools for Learning New Hobbies with AI

These tools assist users in learning new hobbies by offering personalized lessons, real-time feedback, and adaptive learning experiences based on skill level and progress:

- **AIGardenPlanner:** An AI-powered application that provides personalized garden designs and planting plans based on user preferences and garden conditions.
- **Blinkist:** An app that uses AI to summarize non-fiction books into key insights, offering personalized recommendations to help users learn efficiently.

- **Duolingo:** AI-tailored language lessons that adapt to your progress with a gamified approach.
- **Luminar Neo:** A photo editing software that uses AI-driven tools to simplify complex editing tasks, enhance creativity, and deliver professional-quality results for photographers of all levels.
- **Pictory:** AI transforms text into engaging video content, offering a new way to explore video creation.
- **Plantix:** A gardening app that uses AI to diagnose crop issues through photo analysis and provides treatment suggestions to improve plant health.
- **Plant Jammer**: Uses AI to suggest recipes based on ingredients you already have, with a focus on reducing food waste.
- **Procreate Dream:** AI-enhanced tools assist with predictive strokes, color suggestions, and art tutorials.
- **SideChef**: An AI-powered cooking app that offers personalized meal plans, interactive recipes, and tutorials based on users' cooking experience.
- **Skillshare**: An AI-driven platform that recommends courses and tutorials across various creative hobbies such as photography, painting, and graphic design.
- **Yousician**: A musical instrument learning app that provides in-the-moment feedback and adaptive lessons for guitar, piano, and more, tailored to the user's skill level.
- **YouTube**: Uses AI to recommend hobby-related videos, from beginner tutorials to more advanced lessons in any area of interest.

Hands-On Exercise: Exploring a New Hobby with AI

Complexity Rating: 2/5

Estimated Time: 30-45 minutes

1. **Choose a New Hobby**: Pick a hobby you've always wanted to explore, like photography, cooking, painting, or playing a musical instrument—whatever excites you most.
2. **Select an AI-Powered Learning Tool**: Download an app or visit a platform that offers AI-powered lessons or feedback. Check out our suggestions in the *Tools for Learning New Hobbies with AI* section or Google "*AI tool for* [insert your hobby]."
3. **Set Up a Goal:** Establish a simple, clear goal for your chosen hobby, such as learning the basics of guitar chords or cooking three beginner-friendly meals this week.
4. **Start Small:** Use the AI tool to guide you through the first lesson or activity. Focus on how the app customizes your experience, whether through tailored recommendations or interactive feedback.
5. **Track Your Progress**: As you complete your subsequent lessons or tutorials, note how the app tracks your progress and adjusts its recommendations. Use the app's built-in feedback features to improve your skills (if applicable). For instance, **Yousician** provides real-time feedback for music practice, while **Luminar Neo** enhances photos with AI-driven editing tips.
6. **Reflect on Your Experience**: Think about how the AI-guided experience influenced your learning. Did it make the process easier or more engaging? Were the suggestions relevant to your skill level? Consider how you can use AI to continue improving this hobby or explore others in the future.

By following this hands-on exercise, you'll see how AI can simplify the learning process for any new hobby, making it enjoyable and accessible. With the right AI tools guiding you, you'll progress faster and stay more engaged with your chosen passion.

Best Practices for Using AI to Learn a New Hobby:

1. **Consistency is Key**: Commit to practicing regularly for the best results. Whether it's for 15 minutes a day or a couple of hours per week, the more consistent you are, the better AI will adapt to your learning needs and the more skilled you will become at your new hobby.
2. **Leverage AI Feedback**: Many AI-powered tools provide instant feedback. Use this feature, especially in skills like music, photography, or cooking, where precision can enhance your learning experience.
3. **Explore Advanced Features**: As you become more confident with your hobby, explore the app's more advanced features. For example, Yousician's speed exercises can help deepen your skills.

Key Takeaways:

- **AI helps you learn new hobbies at your own pace**: By offering personalized recommendations and feedback, AI makes learning fun, motivating, and tailored to your skill level.
- **Real-time feedback improves skill development**: Whether playing an instrument or editing a photo, AI tools offer immediate insights that help you refine your technique.
- **AI-powered apps adapt as you progress**: As you improve, AI adjusts your lessons, ensuring you grow with the right amount of challenge and without being overwhelmed.

5.4 CREATING A SMART HOME WITH AI: FROM LIGHTS TO LOCKS

Just as AI can help you learn and excel at new hobbies, it can also make life at home easier and more intuitive. Imagine a space where lights, temperature, and security adapt effortlessly to your lifestyle—welcome to the world of AI-powered smart homes.

AI-powered smart home devices can transform your living space into a highly efficient, personalized, and secure environment. From automating lights and temperature controls to securing your home with AI-driven locks and cameras, smart home technology simplifies everyday life and enhances your sense of control. By integrating these devices into a single system, AI creates a seamless experience that responds to your immediate needs.

Automating Your Home with AI

Creating a smart home is about customizing convenience for your desires and needs. You can program your smart devices to follow routines, saving time and reducing energy consumption. For example, smart thermostats like **Nest** learn your daily habits and adjust the temperature based on when you're home or away, ensuring optimal comfort and efficiency.

Similarly, AI-powered lighting systems like **Philips Hue** or **LIFX** allow you to schedule lighting changes based on your preferences. You can create a soothing ambiance by setting the lights to brighten gradually in the morning or dim in the evening, promoting relaxation and supporting your circadian rhythm. Additionally, these systems can be controlled with voice assistants like Alexa or Google Assistant, making adjustments even more convenient.

Enhancing Security with AI

Beyond convenience, AI plays a critical role in home security. AI-driven locks and surveillance cameras, such as **August Smart Lock** and **Ring**, offer real-time monitoring and control whether you're home or not. With AI-powered security cameras, you can receive instant notifications when unexpected movement is detected, while smart locks allow you to lock or unlock your doors remotely from your smartphone.

These systems provide peace of mind, knowing that your home is always under your watchful eye. You can even integrate AI-powered doorbells and cameras with voice assistants, enabling hands-free security management.

As we've seen, smart home devices bring convenience and efficiency to daily life, allowing you to control everything from lights to locks using just your voice or through automated schedules. These devices create an intelligent living environment customized to your lifestyle preferences. Now, let's give it a try and see just how easy it is to set up your own smart home features.

Tools to Help You Create a Smart Home

These tools help users automate and secure their homes, enhancing convenience, energy efficiency, and security through AI-powered devices:

- **Alexa**: A voice assistant that integrates with various smart home devices to control lighting, locks, thermostats, and more through voice commands.
- **August Smart Lock**: An AI-powered smart lock that allows users to lock or unlock their doors remotely via smartphone, enhancing home security.
- **Google Assistant**: Another voice assistant that can control smart home devices, offering similar capabilities to Alexa.
- **LIFX**: An AI-driven lighting system with customizable colors, brightness, and schedules that integrate with voice assistants for hands-free control.
- **Nest**: A smart thermostat that learns your daily habits to adjust temperature settings automatically for optimal comfort and energy savings.
- **Philips Hue**: An AI-powered lighting system that allows users to schedule and control lighting changes through voice assistants like Alexa or Google Assistant.
- **Ring**: AI-driven surveillance cameras and doorbells that offer real-time video monitoring and instant notifications for unexpected activity around your home.

Hands-On Exercise: Setting Up Smart Lights with Alexa

Complexity Rating: 2/5

Estimated Time: 15-20 minutes

1. **Choose Your Smart Lights**: Purchase a set of smart lights, such as **Philips Hue** or **LIFX**, and install them in the room of your choice. Follow the instructions to screw in the bulbs and power them on.
2. **Connect to Your Home Network**: Download the smart lighting app (like Philips Hue or LIFX) and follow the steps to connect the bulbs to your Wi-Fi network. If you have a virtual assistant like **Alexa**, **Google Assistant**, or **Siri**, ensure they're on the same network for easy integration.
3. **Set Up Controls With or Without a Virtual Assistant**:
    - **Using Only the App**: Control smart lights through the app, where you can turn them on or off, adjust brightness, and change colors.
    - **Using a Virtual Assistant**: Open the assistant app (Alexa, Google Assistant, Siri, etc...), navigate to *"Add a new device,"* and select *"Light."* Your assistant will connect to the bulbs for voice control. Try commands like:
        - "Turn on the living room lights."
        - "Dim the bedroom lights to 50%."
        - "Set the kitchen lights to warm white."
4. **Create Lighting Schedules**: In both the lighting app and the virtual assistant app, set routines. For example, schedule the lights to brighten gradually at 7:00 AM or dim at 10:00 PM to support your daily rhythm.

By the end of this exercise, you'll have a fully functional, AI-powered lighting system that enhances the ambiance of your home while adding a layer of convenience. You'll also experience how easily smart devices can be integrated into your home's ecosystem using a voice assistant.

Best Practices for Building a Smart Home:

- **Start Small and Expand**: When creating a smart home, starting with one or two devices, such as smart lights or a thermostat, is best. Once you're comfortable, you can gradually add more devices, like security cameras, smart locks, or even kitchen appliances.
- **Use Routines to Save Energy**: Take advantage of your smart home's scheduling features to save energy. For example, program your lights and thermostat to turn off when you leave for work and turn back on when you return home.
- **Integrate Devices with a Hub**: Use a hub, such as **Amazon Echo** or **Google Nest Hub**, to coordinate all your smart home devices into one ecosystem. This makes managing and controlling everything from your lights to locks much easier and more efficient.

Key Takeaways:

- **AI-powered smart homes enhance convenience and security**: Automating lighting, temperature, and security features streamline daily routines and add peace of mind.
- **Voice assistants make smart home control easy**: With **Alexa**, **Google Assistant**, and similar tools, you can manage your home's lights, locks, and more using simple voice commands.
- **Advanced home security through AI keeps you connected and safe**: AI-enabled locks and cameras offer real-time monitoring and control, ensuring your home's safety whether you're there or away.

Integrating AI into your home allows you to create a personalized and secure living space that adjusts to your daily habits. Smart home devices not only save time but also offer peace of mind by automating routines and providing enhanced security features.

6

LOOKING AHEAD

AI Ethics and Future Trends

As we've discovered throughout this book, AI offers incredible tools to enhance many aspects of our lives, from boosting productivity to simplifying personal tasks. These innovations allow us to achieve more, often with less effort, while opening doors to creativity, convenience, and efficiency. It's easy to get swept up in the excitement of what AI can do for us, and rightfully so.

However, just as AI enhances our daily lives, it also raises more profound, more complex questions about how we interact with these technologies on a broader scale. Beyond its benefits to us personally, AI's impact ripples out across society, influencing areas like privacy, fairness, and even the future of our workforce. Now that you're beginning to master AI's capabilities, it's time to step back and reflect on the bigger picture.

Like any powerful innovation, AI comes with responsibilities. Understanding the broader ethical implications is crucial to ensure that we're not only using AI to our own benefit but also using it thoughtfully, with consideration for long-term consequences. As we move forward, we must also balance progress with accountability. In this chapter, we'll explore the ethical dimensions of AI—equipping you with the knowledge and awareness needed to continue your journey as a savvy and conscientious AI user.

6.1 THE IMPORTANCE OF ETHICAL AI

As AI becomes increasingly embedded into our daily lives, ethical considerations are more imperative than ever. **Ethical AI** goes beyond mere functionality; it involves ensuring fairness, transparency, privacy, and accountability in how AI systems are designed, deployed, and used.

At its core, ethical AI aims to create technology that benefits society while minimizing harm. Developing systems that treat everyone fairly, respect privacy, and ensure transparency in decision-making processes is essential as we advance emerging technologies. We must understand these ethical foundations to ensure responsible and thoughtful use, regardless of how we employ AI tools.

The Foundational Principles of Ethical AI:

- **Fairness:** AI should make decisions that are unbiased and just. Whether recommending products, hiring employees, or assessing credit scores, fairness ensures that AI decisions do not disproportionately favor or discriminate against certain groups.
- **Transparency:** AI systems should be straightforward in their decision-making, providing understandable explanations for reaching conclusions, particularly in critical fields like healthcare and finance.
- **Privacy:** Respect for user privacy is non-negotiable in ethical AI. User data should be protected, and individuals must have control over how their personal information is used.
- **Accountability:** Those who create and use AI systems must take responsibility for their outcomes. If an AI system makes a mistake, there must be a clear accountability chain.

By focusing on these principles, you can make informed decisions about which AI tools to use and how to integrate them into your life in a way that promotes positive outcomes.

6.2 TACKLING BIAS AND FAIRNESS

Bias in AI systems is an increasing concern and is more common than most people realize. When AI is trained on biased data or developed using algorithms that aren't inclusive, it can perpetuate and even amplify societal inequalities. Recognizing and mitigating biases is critical to ensure AI benefits everyone equally.

Types of Bias in AI:

- **Data Bias:** AI systems learn from the data fed to them. If the data is skewed or unrepresentative, the AI's decisions will reflect that bias. For example, if a facial recognition system is trained primarily on lighter-skinned faces, it may have difficulty accurately recognizing people with darker skin tones.
- **Algorithmic Bias:** Sometimes, algorithms are designed to favor one group over another unintentionally. Such outcomes can occur when developers don't account for diverse user needs or fail to test the algorithm in various contexts.
- **Societal Bias:** AI systems don't operate in a vacuum; they mirror the biases in the societies that create them. For example, hiring algorithms that favor certain types of resumes may reinforce existing societal biases related to gender or education.

While bias in AI is a growing concern, it's important to remember that addressing these challenges also opens up a world of possibility and opportunity. By being proactive and thoughtful in how we develop and use AI, we can build systems that are more inclusive, fair, and beneficial to everyone. The potential for AI to uplift individuals and communities is vast, and with the right strategies in place, we can ensure that AI serves as a force for positive change. Together, we can work toward an AI-driven future that empowers everyone–regardless of background or identity.

Strategies for Reducing Bias:

- **Diverse and Representative Datasets:** Ensuring that the data used to train AI systems is diverse and representative of different genders, races, and socio-economic backgrounds is one of the most effective ways to reduce bias.
- **Algorithm Transparency:** Developers should clearly explain how AI algorithms function, and provide insight into their decision-making processes to foster accountability and trust.
- **Regular Audits and Updates:** Bias can emerge over time, so regular audits and updates are essential to keeping AI systems fair and inclusive.

Implementing these strategies will significantly minimize bias in AI systems and ensure the technology serves all users equitably.

However, fairness is just one piece of the bigger puzzle. As AI continues to evolve, protecting personal data is another crucial aspect to consider. Responsible data handling is at the core of ethical AI, especially in an age where privacy concerns are growing. In the next section, we'll explore how safeguarding user privacy is necessary to build trust and secure the long-term success of AI technologies.

6.3 DATA PRIVACY IN THE AGE OF AI

AI systems frequently depend on large amounts of personal data to function effectively, raising important questions about how data is collected, stored, and used. Ethical AI systems uphold privacy guidelines by responsibly safeguarding and handling users' personal information.

How AI Uses Your Data

To provide personalized experiences, AI applications like virtual assistants, smart home devices, and health trackers rely on user data. This information can include everything from your location and browsing history to health information and spending habits. While these details make AI tools more effective, they also introduce privacy risks when mishandled.

Best Practices for Data Privacy:

- **Anonymization:** AI systems should anonymize personal data to protect individuals' identities.
- **Data Minimization:** Only necessary data should be collected, and this data should only be used for its intended purpose.
- **Informed Consent:** Users should be overtly informed of how their data is being used and have the choice to opt out at any time.

While it's essential for AI developers to implement best practices like anonymization, data minimization, and informed consent, protecting your privacy also requires active participation and accountability. As a user, you can make informed decisions about how your data is handled. By understanding how AI tools operate and taking a few simple precautions, you can keep your personal information safe and secure while enjoying the benefits of AI's convenience and innovation.

How to Protect Your Data:

- **Review Privacy Settings**: Always check the privacy settings of any AI tool. Most applications have data-sharing options that you can adjust to your comfort level.
- **Read Privacy Policies**: Before using any AI application, take a moment to review its privacy policy. Understand what data is being collected and how it will be used. If you're uncomfortable with the terms, look for alternative tools that better align with your privacy needs.

- **Use Strong Passwords and Two-Factor Authentication**: Protect your accounts with strong, unique passwords, and enable two-factor authentication (2FA) whenever possible, adding an extra layer of security.
- **Be Selective with Sharing**: Only provide the minimum amount of personal information required by the AI system. If an app asks you for more data than seems necessary, reconsider using it.
- **Regularly Update Software**: Keep your AI tools and devices updated with the latest security features and patches.

As you take steps to protect your personal data and make informed decisions about the AI tools you use, it's equally important to consider who is responsible when things go wrong. Accountability is just as important as privacy and security when it comes to ethics. Next, we'll navigate the complexities of defining responsibility in the evolving AI landscape. As AI systems make decisions with real-world consequences, understanding who to hold accountable is crucial for maintaining ethical and fair outcomes.

6.4 ACCOUNTABILITY IN AI: WHO'S RESPONSIBLE?

One of the most intriguing questions regarding AI is how to establish accountability. Identifying responsibility for AI is crucial, whether it's used to approve a loan, diagnose a medical condition, or predict criminal outcomes. How do we verify that AI systems aren't left unchecked and that those who develop and use these tools are held accountable for their decisions?

The Challenge of Accountability

In traditional systems, it's obvious when a mistake is made who the responsible person is. However, with AI, responsibility is often dispersed and shared between developers, users, and organizations. For example, if an AI system incorrectly denies someone a loan, is it the fault of the algorithm's developer, the company that deployed the AI, or the person who relied on its decision?

Best Practices for AI Accountability:

- **Clear Roles and Responsibilities:** Companies using AI should clearly define who is responsible for monitoring AI and correcting when AI makes errors.
- **Human Oversight:** AI systems should only operate with some degree of human oversight, especially in high-stakes situations.
- **Regular Reviews:** Companies must regularly review AI systems to ensure ethical decisions are being made and promptly take corrective actions when mistakes occur.

Accountability in AI is fundamental to maintaining public trust and ensuring these systems benefit society ethically. While it may seem complex, there are steps you can take to interact with and implement AI systems responsibly. As AI evolves, remember that both companies and individuals play a role in ensuring accountability—so take action and do your part.

Empowering Individual Accountability in AI

Here's how you can contribute to a culture of responsibility:

- **Ask the Right Questions**: Whether you're using AI tools at work or in your personal life, don't be afraid to ask questions about how decisions are made and who is responsible for them. Understanding the layers of oversight and how errors are corrected can help you trust the technology.
- **Seek Transparency**: Companies should be transparent about their AI systems, including how they make decisions and who takes responsibility for outcomes. Look for companies that are open about their AI practices and prioritize ethical use.
- **Hold Companies Accountable**: Take action if you encounter an issue with an AI system—whether it's a misjudged credit score or an unfair recommendation. Contact the company, ask for an explanation, and expect

accountability. Ethical companies will welcome this feedback and take steps to improve their systems.
- **Stay Informed**: As AI technology evolves, so does the conversation around accountability. Keep up with new regulations, industry best practices, and updates on how experts address AI accountability. Staying informed empowers you to make better decisions and advocate for fairer systems.

By staying engaged, asking the right questions, and demanding transparency, you can play an active role in ensuring AI systems are used responsibly. Accountability is not just a challenge for developers and stakeholders—it's an opportunity for all of us to shape how AI impacts the world for the better.

6.5 THE FUTURE OF AI: WHAT'S NEXT?

As we've explored, AI's ethical challenges—privacy, bias, and accountability—are necessary considerations as we integrate this technology more deeply into society. However, alongside these challenges lies immense potential. AI is not just a tool for today; it's a catalyst for tomorrow's innovations. AI is becoming more intelligent, transparent, and intuitive with each new advancement. Now, let's look beyond the hurdles to the exciting developments shaping AI's future and how they will continue to enhance our lives.

The future of AI is filled with possibilities that are not only exciting but transformative. As AI continues to evolve, we're on the cusp of advancements that will reshape industries, enhance daily life, and address many of the challenges we've encountered so far. These innovations are not a distant prospect—they are emerging now, promising a future where AI is more transparent, efficient, and seamlessly integrated into our world. With each breakthrough, AI will become more accessible, understandable, and ultimately more empowering for everyone.

Key Emerging Trends:

- **Explainable AI (XAI)**: One of the most promising developments is the rise of explainable AI, which focuses on transparency. Imagine being able to ask an AI system not just for a decision but for a clear explanation of *how* it arrived there. This shift is particularly beneficial in high-stakes industries like healthcare and finance, where understanding the "why" behind an AI's choice can lead to better outcomes and greater trust.
- **Edge AI**: Another exciting trend is edge AI, where data processing happens on local devices rather than in the cloud. This means faster, on-the-spot results with enhanced privacy protection. As edge AI grows, expect to see it revolutionize smart homes, autonomous vehicles, and Internet of Things (IoT) devices, making them more responsive and efficient without sacrificing security.
- **AI in Augmented Reality (AR) and Virtual Reality (VR)**: AI is also set to transform how we experience augmented and virtual realities. By powering more innovative, immersive AR and VR environments, AI will enhance fields such as gaming, education, and professional training. Imagine AI-guided virtual classrooms or training simulations so lifelike that they redefine how we learn and work.

Opportunities and Challenges

The potential for AI to innovate and improve lives is immense. From revolutionizing healthcare diagnostics and personalizing education to enhancing everyday conveniences, AI is rapidly pushing the boundaries of what's possible. As these technologies become more embedded in society, the potential to address real-world challenges is more significant than ever.

Of course, with these advancements come responsibilities. Ensuring that AI evolves ethically, addressing biases, and protecting privacy are critical areas that will guide the future of its development. However, the exciting news is that as AI advances, the tools and frameworks that help reinforce its responsible use advance as well.

By staying informed and engaged with these emerging trends, you'll be well-prepared to confidently embrace the future of AI. With thoughtful innovation and oversight, AI can potentially create a more connected, equitable, and forward-thinking world.

7

EXTENDED PRACTICAL GUIDE

Mastering ChatGPT for Everyday Life with 350 Prompts and Meta-Prompts

7.1 HOW TO USE THE EXTENDED PRACTICAL GUIDE

Now that you've explored the incredible versatility of ChatGPT,it's time to expand your skills by applying them to everyday scenarios. In this *Extended Practical Guide*, you'll find prompts covering a wide range of categories, helping you tackle everything from career development to creativity and personal growth. Here's a glimpse of the areas we'll explore together:

- Time Management and Productivity
- Personal Finance
- Career Development
- Health and Wellness
- Relationship Building
- Self-Improvement and Mindfulness
- Entrepreneurship and Business Strategy
- Leadership
- Learning and Education
- Automating Routine Tasks
- Creative Problem-Solving

- Financial Growth
- ... and many more!

How to Use This Guide

This *Extended Practical Guide* includes both ready-made prompts you can use immediately and guidance on creating your own. Here's how to approach each section and make the most of the tools provided:

- **Start with the Provided Prompts:** Each section begins with ten pre-scripted prompts tailored to specific areas. These prompts are designed to give you instant, actionable solutions. You can simply copy a prompt, customize the placeholder details like [project] or [task], and let ChatGPT guide you through your next steps.
- **Tailor Prompts to Your Needs:** If a prompt feels too generic or doesn't quite fit your exact scenario, don't hesitate to modify it. Add more context, specific tasks, or time frames to help ChatGPT provide a response that aligns with your unique goals. Think of the provided prompts as templates you can tweak to suit your personal or professional situation.
- **Layer Prompts for a Holistic Approach:** You can also combine prompts across different categories. For example, start with a time management prompt to organize your day, then add a self-improvement prompt to include personal development goals. This layering technique allows you to approach your personal and professional life in a balanced, integrated way.
- **Use Meta-Prompts to Go Deeper:** You'll find a meta-prompt after the ten pre-scripted prompts in each section. Meta-prompts are designed to help you craft more dynamic, personalized prompts. They invite you to go deeper, refine your goals, and gain more control over the outputs you receive. Using meta-prompts allows you to tailor ChatGPT's responses to be even more specific to your needs, making it a more powerful tool.

- **Experiment and Iterate:** Finally, remember that the first result may not always be the perfect fit. The beauty of AI is its flexibility. Feel free to adjust your prompts based on the responses you get. You can rephrase, add more details, or try a completely different approach. The goal is to refine your interactions with ChatGPT so the responses align more closely with your needs.

Best Practices for Crafting Prompts and Meta-Prompts

As you dive into these prompts, keep the following best practices in mind to ensure you're getting the most out of ChatGPT:

- **Be Specific**: The more context and details you provide, the better ChatGPT can tailor its responses to your needs.
- **Focus on One Task at a Time**: Keep prompts focused on a single task or goal to ensure clarity and precision.
- **Provide Examples When Needed**: If you have a particular format or style in mind, include an example to guide ChatGPT's output.
- **State the Desired Outcome**: Clearly describe what you want ChatGPT to deliver, whether it's a schedule, a summary, or suggestions.

7.2 350 PRACTICAL PROMPTS AND META-PROMPTS

Time Management and Productivity

1. Create a daily schedule for me that balances focused work, breaks, and personal activities. Ensure it includes [project 1], [project 2], and time for self-care activities like walking or meditation. Prioritize my most important tasks first thing in the morning.
2. Set up a detailed weekly planner with deadlines for [ongoing project 1], [ongoing project 2], and include buffer time for unexpected tasks. Each task should be assigned to a specific day and time block for high-priority work.

3. Break down my [specific project] into actionable steps with estimated time for each task. I need this organized to show me how to complete the project within [time frame], and I would like suggestions for how I can stay on track.
4. Generate a time-blocking schedule for tomorrow that focuses on my top three priorities: [priority task 1], [priority task 2], and [priority task 3]. Ensure there's time for breaks and end-of-day reflection on progress.
5. Suggest specific strategies to reduce distractions and improve focus during my [3-hour focused work session] on [project]. Recommend any tools or techniques I can use to block distractions, and include short break intervals to keep productivity high.
6. Create a morning routine that boosts productivity, including 15 minutes for planning my day, time for a healthy breakfast, and setting intentions. I'd also like to incorporate a 10-minute stretch or quick exercise to start the day with energy.
7. Develop an evening routine that helps me wind down after a long day, including tasks like reviewing my progress, planning for the next day, and incorporating a 30-minute activity for relaxation, like reading or meditating.
8. Recommend three productivity apps that can help me stay organized, track my time, and set reminders. Ensure that these apps can sync across my devices and help me manage both work and personal tasks effectively.
9. Plan my upcoming week, accounting for [upcoming deadline] on [day], [meeting] on [day], and personal commitments like [event]. Make sure I have time to prepare for meetings and finish key tasks without feeling overwhelmed.
10. Suggest specific strategies for prioritizing tasks when I feel overwhelmed. Help me figure out which tasks to tackle first, what can be delegated, and how to manage my energy to stay productive throughout the day.
11. **Meta-Prompt:** Create a prompt that helps me design a personalized daily schedule, incorporating [specific tasks like meetings, creative work, or exercise] and balancing time for

[self-care, family, relaxation]. Ensure it optimizes productivity while reducing burnout.

Personal Finance

12. Create a monthly budget for me, including categories like housing, groceries, entertainment, and savings, ensuring I have a surplus for investing.
13. Suggest a savings plan to help me build an emergency fund over the next 6 months, based on my current income and expenses.
14. Analyze my spending habits and recommend areas where I can cut unnecessary expenses to increase my monthly savings.
15. Generate a 5-year financial plan that includes paying off debt, building an emergency fund, investing, and saving for retirement.
16. Provide a diversified investment strategy based on moderate risk tolerance, including a combination of stocks, bonds, real estate options, and other investments.
17. Recommend a step-by-step plan for saving for a major purchase, like a home or car, while maintaining my current financial obligations.
18. Set up a monthly system to track my financial goals and review progress, focusing on savings and debt reduction.
19. Suggest a retirement savings plan, considering my current age, income, and desired retirement lifestyle.
20. Create a strategy for managing irregular income (e.g., freelance work) while maintaining consistent savings and debt payments.
21. **Meta-Prompt:** Generate a prompt that guides me through creating a customized monthly budget, ensuring it includes [income streams, expenses, and savings goals]. Include tips for prioritizing essential expenses and planning for long-term financial goals.

Career Development

22. Create a tailored resume for a [specific job title] position, highlighting my skills in [key skills like leadership, data analysis, project management, etc.] and recent achievements in [specific accomplishments like project completions, sales growth, or awards].
23. Suggest networking strategies for advancing my career in the [specific industry like tech, healthcare, finance, etc.], focusing on building meaningful connections with industry leaders and peers through [platforms like LinkedIn or industry conferences].
24. Develop a list of action steps to enhance my LinkedIn profile, including specific recommendations for updating my [headline, summary, skills section, and endorsements] to align with my career goals in [specific industry or role].
25. Break down my job search process into manageable tasks, including [researching companies, customizing resumes, drafting cover letters, preparing for interviews], and suggesting a timeline for each task.
26. Generate a list of potential companies or job titles that align with my experience in [specific areas like marketing, sales, software engineering, etc.], helping me target my job search more effectively.
27. Create a plan to improve my public speaking skills, including weekly exercises like [practicing speeches, attending Toastmasters, recording and reviewing presentations], and recommending resources like [courses, books, or online tutorials].
28. Suggest strategies for improving my personal brand online, focusing on [content creation, sharing industry insights, and engaging with thought leaders on platforms like LinkedIn or Twitter] to increase my visibility in the [specific industry].
29. Develop a plan to transition into a leadership role in my current company, including action steps like [seeking

mentorship, taking on more responsibilities, or enhancing key leadership skills like communication and decision-making].

30. Suggest ways to balance continuous learning with my current job responsibilities in [specific role or industry], providing ideas for [online courses, certifications, or skills development] that will keep me competitive.
31. Create a one-page career development plan that outlines my short-term goals (within 6 months) and long-term goals (within 2-5 years) for advancing in my field of [specific industry], with deadlines for achieving each.
32. **Meta-Prompt:** Write a prompt that helps me build a resume tailored to a [specific job position or industry], highlighting my [skills, experience, and achievements]. Include suggestions for optimizing the format for applicant tracking systems (ATS).

Health and Wellness

33. Create a weekly workout plan for me, including [strength training, cardio, and flexibility exercises] that fit within my schedule of [specific days and available time, e.g., 3 days a week, 45 minutes each session].
34. Create a personalized meal plan that focuses on [specific dietary goals like weight loss, muscle gain, or maintaining energy levels], with [breakfast, lunch, dinner, and snacks] based on [specific preferences, e.g., low-carb, high-protein, plant-based].
35. Generate a morning routine that prioritizes both physical and mental wellness, including [stretching, meditation, and hydration] within [specific time frame, e.g., 30 minutes after waking up].
36. Suggest relaxation and stress management techniques that can fit into my daily routine, especially during [stressful times like after work or before bed], including [deep breathing exercises, mindfulness meditation, or progressive muscle relaxation].

37. Create a 30-day fitness challenge that gradually increases in difficulty, focusing on [specific goals like increasing endurance, strength, or flexibility] with a weekly review of progress.
38. Suggest a daily water intake schedule based on my activity level and body weight of [insert weight], incorporating reminders to drink water throughout the day using [apps like WaterMinder or reminders through my phone].
39. Develop a personalized sleep improvement plan that helps me fall asleep faster and wake up with energy, focusing on [bedtime routines like limiting screen time, reading, or practicing relaxation techniques].
40. Recommend specific mindfulness or meditation practices that I can incorporate into my daily life to reduce stress and improve focus, especially during [specific times like before a big meeting or after work].
41. Create a recovery plan for me after an intense workout or sports event, including [hydration, stretching, and rest days], with tips on how to avoid injury and maintain overall wellness.
42. Suggest a combination of physical activities, such as [yoga, jogging, strength training, or cycling], to help me stay motivated and avoid burnout, ensuring a balance of variety and consistency in my fitness routine.
43. **Meta-Prompt:** Create a prompt to generate a weekly fitness plan that considers [my fitness goals like weight loss or strength training] and [specific activities like yoga, HIIT, or running]. Suggest how I can monitor progress and stay motivated.

Relationship Building

44. Suggest conversation starters that can help me strengthen my relationships with [specific people, e.g., my spouse, family, or coworkers], especially in [specific settings, e.g., during dinner, on weekends, or during work breaks].
45. Develop a weekly check-in system for staying connected with [friends, family, or coworkers] through [text, phone calls, or

video chats], including reminders to reach out and specific questions to ask about their well-being.

46. Create a plan for improving communication in my relationship with [insert person's name, e.g., spouse, partner, or colleague], focusing on [active listening, empathy, and understanding each other's needs].
47. Provide actionable steps for resolving conflicts in my relationship with [insert person], focusing on [specific issues like miscommunication or disagreements about priorities].
48. Suggest a monthly relationship-building activity for [my partner or family], including [date night ideas, group activities, or family outings] that foster deeper connections.
49. Recommend ways to express gratitude and appreciation to [specific people, e.g., partner, coworkers, or friends] on a regular basis, including [small gestures, written notes, or acts of service].
50. Create a strategy for improving my teamwork and collaboration skills at work, focusing on [active communication, sharing ideas, and supporting team members during projects].
51. Develop a plan for creating more meaningful connections with new people in my life, focusing on [specific social settings like networking events or casual meetups].
52. Suggest ways to improve my emotional intelligence and empathy when dealing with [specific relationships, e.g., a difficult coworker, my partner, or a family member].
53. Create a system for remembering important dates (e.g., birthdays or anniversaries) and setting reminders for celebrating or acknowledging these moments with [specific people in your life].
54. **Meta-Prompt:** Develop a prompt that helps me write personalized messages to strengthen relationships with [friends, family, or colleagues], ensuring it includes [expressing gratitude, scheduling quality time, or resolving conflicts] in a thoughtful manner.

Self-Improvement and Mindfulness

55. Create a 30-day habit-building plan for developing a daily mindfulness meditation routine, including suggestions for [morning or evening sessions] and tips for staying consistent.
56. Suggest a personalized morning affirmation routine that helps me focus on [specific personal goals, such as reducing stress, increasing confidence, or building gratitude].
57. Develop a self-reflection practice for me to follow at the end of each day, including [journaling prompts or questions like "What did I learn today?" or "How can I improve tomorrow?"].
58. Create a step-by-step plan for introducing mindfulness practices into my workday, including [mindful breaks, breathing exercises, and stress-relief techniques].
59. Suggest a list of 5-minute mindfulness activities I can incorporate into my busy schedule, focusing on [improving focus, reducing stress, or boosting creativity].
60. Help me create a gratitude journaling habit, including prompts like "What am I grateful for today?" and "What small wins did I have this week?"
61. Provide a weekly self-care plan that incorporates [yoga, meditation, or creative hobbies], ensuring I make time for myself amidst my busy schedule.
62. Create a system for tracking my personal growth over the next 6 months, including [monthly check-ins or progress reviews on specific habits or goals].
63. Suggest a personalized evening routine that helps me wind down after work and transition into relaxation mode, including activities like [reading, meditation, or reflection].
64. Provide prompts for a weekly journaling practice focused on personal growth, covering areas such as [self-awareness, emotional health, and setting intentions for the future].
65. **Meta-Prompt:** Generate a prompt for creating a 30-day habit-building plan focused on [personal development areas

like mindfulness, gratitude, or goal-setting]. Include strategies for tracking progress and staying consistent.

Entrepreneurship and Business Strategy

66. Generate five business ideas in the [industry of your choice], incorporating trends like [sustainability, digital transformation, or AI].
67. Break down the steps needed to create a business plan for [your business idea], including sections like market research, financial projections, and marketing strategies.
68. Suggest a competitive analysis framework for [your industry or business], focusing on identifying key competitors, analyzing their strengths and weaknesses, and finding market gaps.
69. Create a one-page business strategy outline for my [specific business idea], covering areas like value proposition, target audience, and revenue model.
70. Provide a market research plan for validating a new product idea in the [specific industry], including steps like surveys, focus groups, and analyzing customer behavior.
71. Suggest a pricing strategy for my [product or service], considering factors like cost of goods sold, market competition, and customer willingness to pay.
72. Help me outline a pitch deck for investors, focusing on key sections like problem statement, solution, market opportunity, and financial projections for [your business].
73. Create a checklist for launching a new product, including tasks like [market testing, creating marketing materials, and coordinating with suppliers].
74. Suggest five marketing campaign ideas for a [new product or service] launch, targeting [specific audiences] and using channels like [social media, email, or influencer marketing].
75. Outline a 90-day plan for growing my business, including tasks like [customer acquisition, refining operations, and building partnerships].

76. **Meta-Prompt:** Create a prompt that guides me in brainstorming innovative business ideas for the [specific industry or niche]. Ensure the prompt includes researching market trends, understanding customer challenges, and crafting a compelling value proposition.

Leadership

77. Create a 30-day leadership development plan, including daily tasks to improve communication, decision-making, and team management skills.
78. Suggest strategies for building trust and transparency within my team, particularly when working remotely or across different time zones.
79. Generate a list of leadership qualities I should focus on developing to be more effective in [specific role, like project manager, team leader, or department head].
80. Provide actionable steps for handling difficult conversations with team members about [specific issues like underperformance, conflicts, or setting expectations].
81. Recommend ways to motivate and inspire my team during challenging projects, including methods for recognizing individual contributions and fostering a positive culture.
82. Create a leadership meeting agenda for a weekly team check-in, focusing on [specific goals like reviewing progress, setting priorities, or addressing challenges].
83. Suggest strategies for mentoring and developing future leaders within my organization, including practical ways to empower team members to take the initiative.
84. Generate a list of techniques to improve decision-making under pressure, ensuring I make thoughtful and effective choices during high-stakes situations.
85. Provide a framework for conducting performance reviews that focus on both constructive feedback and actionable development plans for each team member.

86. Recommend ways to enhance cross-department collaboration and ensure alignment on key organizational goals, including strategies for fostering open communication.
87. **Meta-Prompt:** Write a prompt to help me improve my delegation skills as a leader, including suggestions for [prioritizing tasks, assigning responsibilities to team members, and tracking progress effectively].

Learning and Education

88. Create a study plan for learning [subject or skill, like Python programming], including recommended resources, practice exercises, and a weekly schedule.
89. Suggest daily learning activities to improve my [specific skill, like public speaking], with a focus on building confidence and engaging with an audience.
90. Break down the steps needed to master [specific concept or subject] over the next month, including reading materials, practical exercises, and review sessions.
91. Recommend online courses or platforms for learning [specific skill, like graphic design], with a focus on beginner-friendly options that offer hands-on practice.
92. Create a personalized learning roadmap for [specific goal, like becoming proficient in data science], including milestones and key concepts to cover each week.
93. Suggest effective study techniques for retaining information on [specific subject], including active recall, spaced repetition, and self-testing.
94. Develop a weekly reading plan to stay updated on [specific industry or topic], recommending sources like articles, journals, or newsletters.
95. Suggest interactive tools or apps for learning [specific language or skill], and provide strategies for practicing daily.
96. Create a plan for improving my critical thinking and problem-solving skills through [specific activities or challenges], with weekly goals and exercises.

97. Recommend strategies for balancing learning with a busy schedule, ensuring I make steady progress in mastering [specific skill or subject].
98. **Meta-Prompt:** Write a prompt that helps me create a study plan for mastering [specific skill or subject], ensuring it includes [daily practice, review sessions, and resource recommendations] to help me stay on track and measure progress.

Cooking and Recipes

99. Create a meal plan for the week using [specific dietary preferences, like vegetarian or keto], including breakfast, lunch, dinner, and snacks.
100. Suggest recipes using [specific ingredients you have at home, like chicken, spinach, and rice], focusing on quick and easy options.
101. Plan a themed dinner menu for [specific occasion, like a birthday or holiday], including appetizers, main course, and dessert.
102. Generate healthy lunch ideas that take less than 30 minutes to prepare, focusing on [specific needs, like high-protein or low-carb].
103. Suggest creative ways to use leftovers from [specific meal, like roast chicken or pasta], to reduce food waste and make new dishes.
104. Provide step-by-step instructions for cooking [specific dish, like lasagna or stir-fry], including tips for enhancing flavor and presentation.
105. Plan a grocery list based on [your weekly meal plan or specific recipes], ensuring I have all the necessary ingredients.
106. Recommend beginner-friendly cooking techniques for mastering [specific skill, like grilling or sautéing], including practical tips.

107. Suggest easy meal prep strategies for the week to help me stay on track with my [specific health goals, like weight loss or muscle gain].
108. Create a themed menu for a [specific event, like a summer BBQ or dinner party], with easy-to-follow recipes and beverage pairings.
109. **Meta-Prompt:** Generate a prompt that helps me create a personalized weekly meal plan, including [specific dietary preferences, available ingredients, and nutritional goals]. Include tips for making the meal prep efficient and enjoyable.

Automating Routine Tasks

110. Set up a daily reminder system using [Google Calendar, Todoist, or other apps] to track important tasks and deadlines.
111. Suggest a weekly automation workflow for managing my [emails, social media posts, or client communications], focusing on time-saving strategies.
112. Create an automated schedule for sending [meeting invitations, project updates, or follow-up emails] using [specific tools, like Calendly or HubSpot].
113. Automate my personal finance management by setting up automatic [bill payments, savings transfers, or budget tracking] with [specific apps like Pocketguard or YNAB].
114. Develop a system for automatically backing up my important files using [cloud storage solutions, like Google Drive or Dropbox].
115. Set up an automatic reminder system for recurring tasks, such as [paying bills, scheduling medical appointments, or reviewing financial statements].
116. Automate the process of tracking my daily [fitness goals, water intake, or sleep patterns] using [health apps like Fitbit or Apple Health].
117. Create an automated task management system that tracks my progress on [ongoing projects, work tasks, or personal goals], using [tools like Trello or Asana].

118. Schedule automatic check-ins with [clients, team members, or family] to maintain regular communication and ensure progress is being made.
119. Automate my social media posting schedule for [specific platforms, like Instagram, LinkedIn, or Twitter], using [tools like Hootsuite or Buffer].
120. **Meta-Prompt:** Develop a prompt that helps me automate my daily tasks using [specific apps or tools like Notion, Google Calendar, or Zapier], ensuring that I can track reminders, set deadlines, and streamline my workflow effectively.

Creative Problem-Solving

121. Suggest innovative solutions for improving [specific work challenge, like team productivity or client retention], including actionable steps.
122. Brainstorm new ways to tackle [specific project or personal challenge], focusing on creative approaches and out-of-the-box thinking.
123. Generate a list of alternative solutions for [specific problem, like budget cuts or tight deadlines], considering potential risks and rewards.
124. Create a step-by-step action plan to overcome [specific obstacle or roadblock], with clear goals and milestones for success.
125. Suggest creative ways to streamline [specific process, like onboarding new clients or managing team workflows], ensuring maximum efficiency.
126. Provide strategies for encouraging more innovative thinking in [specific team or department], including tips for fostering collaboration and idea-sharing.
127. Break down [specific problem] into smaller, more manageable parts, and suggest solutions for each one.
128. Recommend brainstorming techniques to generate fresh ideas for [specific project or task], ensuring a diverse range of creative possibilities.

129. Create a list of potential improvements for [specific product or service], based on current market trends and customer feedback.
130. Suggest strategies for overcoming creative blocks and boosting my problem-solving abilities when working on [specific tasks or projects].
131. **Meta-Prompt:** Write a prompt that assists me in brainstorming creative solutions for [specific challenge or project], encouraging innovative thinking by incorporating different perspectives and strategies for overcoming obstacles.

Financial Growth

132. Create a personalized investment strategy based on [specific financial goals, risk tolerance, and time horizon].
133. Suggest profitable side hustle ideas for someone with [specific skills or interests, like graphic design, writing, or coding].
134. Develop a plan for increasing my passive income through [investments, real estate, or digital products], focusing on sustainable growth.
135. Recommend strategies for maximizing my retirement savings, including options for [IRAs, 401(k)s, or other retirement accounts].
136. Break down the steps needed to start investing in [specific assets, like stocks, bonds, or cryptocurrency], including platforms and strategies.
137. Suggest ways to diversify my investment portfolio, ensuring a balance between [high-risk and low-risk assets].
138. Create a long-term savings plan for [specific goal, like retirement, buying a house or starting a business], with monthly contributions and milestones.
139. Provide actionable strategies for paying off [specific debts, like student loans or credit card debt], focusing on debt reduction and financial freedom.
140. Suggest tools for tracking my net worth and financial growth, ensuring I stay on track with [specific financial goals].

141. Recommend tax-saving strategies for [self-employed individuals, small business owners, or investors], to minimize liabilities and maximize returns.
142. **Meta-Prompt:** Create a prompt that helps me develop a long-term investment strategy based on [my risk tolerance, financial goals, and market preferences], ensuring that it includes [diversified investments, savings targets, and risk mitigation strategies].

Saving Time with Technology

143. Recommend time-saving apps and tools for managing [projects, client communications, or daily tasks], ensuring I stay organized and efficient.
144. Create a system for automating my [email responses, social media management, or calendar scheduling] using AI-driven tools.
145. Suggest shortcuts and time-saving techniques for improving my workflow in [specific software or tool, like Excel, Photoshop, or Google Sheets].
146. Develop a strategy for streamlining my daily tasks, including [automation, delegation, and prioritization techniques].
147. Recommend tools for automating data entry and analysis, reducing manual work and improving accuracy in [specific tasks, like accounting or research].
148. Create a plan for minimizing distractions and improving focus during work, using [specific productivity tools or techniques, like time-blocking or the Pomodoro method].
149. Suggest AI tools for streamlining my client communications, ensuring I stay responsive without spending too much time on emails.
150. Develop a strategy for reducing repetitive tasks in [specific role or department], focusing on automation and efficiency.
151. Create a streamlined digital filing system for organizing [important documents, client files, or project materials] using [specific tools, like Google Drive or Notion].

152. Recommend ways to automate my daily planning and scheduling, ensuring I stay on top of [meetings, deadlines, and personal commitments].
153. **Meta-Prompt:** Generate a prompt that suggests the best AI tools and apps for streamlining [specific tasks like project management, data entry, or content creation], ensuring they save time and increase efficiency.

Home and Family Life

154. Create a weekly cleaning schedule for [specific family size, like a family of four], ensuring tasks are evenly distributed among all members.
155. Plan a family weekend itinerary with [specific activities for kids and adults, like hiking, museum visits, or movie nights], ensuring everyone has fun.
156. Suggest ways to improve home organization, focusing on [specific areas like decluttering, storage solutions, or creating functional spaces].
157. Develop a system for managing family schedules and appointments, using [specific apps or tools, like Google Calendar or Cozi].
158. Recommend strategies for creating more quality family time, including [weekly family dinners, game nights, or outdoor activities].
159. Create a plan for organizing [specific areas in the home, like the kitchen, garage, or living room], ensuring everything is easily accessible.
160. Suggest ways to teach children about responsibility and time management, including [age-appropriate chores, reward systems, or educational tools].
161. Plan a family budget that accounts for [groceries, entertainment, travel, and savings], ensuring financial stability and reducing unnecessary spending.
162. Develop strategies for balancing family time with personal and professional responsibilities, ensuring no area is neglected.

163. Recommend tools for organizing family tasks, such as [digital chore charts, shared calendars, or reminder apps], to keep everyone on track.
164. **Meta-Prompt:** Write a prompt that helps me create a weekly family schedule, balancing [household tasks, family activities, and work commitments], ensuring everyone has roles and responsibilities while maintaining time for relaxation.

Social Connection and Networking

165. Generate icebreaker questions for [specific type of event, like a virtual networking event, family gathering, or professional conference], ensuring engaging conversations.
166. Suggest creative ways to stay connected with [long-distance friends or family], including [regular video calls, shared hobbies, or group chats].
167. Develop strategies for expanding my professional network in [specific industry or field, like marketing, tech, or finance], focusing on [LinkedIn, conferences, or mentorship opportunities].
168. Plan a virtual networking event with [specific goals, like connecting with industry leaders or growing your client base], ensuring meaningful connections.
169. Suggest strategies for maintaining strong relationships with colleagues, including [regular check-ins, team-building activities, or professional development sessions].
170. Create a plan for attending [specific conferences, workshops, or industry events], focusing on networking opportunities and career growth.
171. Suggest ways to improve communication with [specific group, like coworkers, clients, or family], focusing on active listening and empathy.
172. Develop a strategy for building deeper connections with [specific group, like friends, family, or coworkers], ensuring meaningful and lasting relationships.

173. Create a plan for reconnecting with old friends or colleagues, including [sending catch-up emails, organizing meetups, or collaborating on projects].
174. Recommend strategies for building a personal brand on [specific social media platforms, like LinkedIn or Twitter], ensuring visibility and connection with others.
175. **Meta-Prompt:** Create a prompt that helps me develop a personalized networking strategy, ensuring it includes [specific events or platforms like LinkedIn, networking events, or industry forums] to build meaningful connections.

Emotional Intelligence and Well-being

176. Provide tips for improving emotional intelligence in the workplace, focusing on [self-awareness, empathy, and effective communication].
177. Create a daily routine for maintaining emotional well-being, including [mindfulness exercises, gratitude practices, and reflection].
178. Suggest ways to handle stressful situations at work, focusing on [conflict resolution, emotional regulation, and self-care].
179. Develop a plan for improving empathy in [specific relationships, like with coworkers, family, or friends], focusing on active listening and understanding.
180. Suggest relaxation techniques for reducing stress, including [deep breathing exercises, yoga, or guided meditation].
181. Provide ideas or options for maintaining a healthy work-life balance, ensuring I avoid burnout while staying productive in [specific tasks or responsibilities].
182. Create a daily journaling practice to improve emotional well-being, including [prompts for reflection, gratitude, and goal setting].
183. Suggest ways to improve emotional regulation during high-stress situations, including [specific techniques, like mindfulness or cognitive reframing].

184. Develop a plan for building emotional resilience, ensuring I can handle challenges in [specific areas of life, like work, relationships, or personal growth].
185. Provide strategies for nurturing positive relationships with [specific people, like coworkers, friends, or family], focusing on emotional intelligence and empathy.
186. **Meta-Prompt:** Develop a prompt that guides me through creating a daily mindfulness routine, focusing on [specific areas like stress reduction, gratitude, or self-awareness], ensuring that it fits seamlessly into my daily life.

Sustainability and Minimalism

187. Suggest eco-friendly practices for reducing household waste, including [composting, recycling, and reducing single-use plastics].
188. Create a step-by-step guide for decluttering my home, focusing on [one room at a time, starting with the kitchen or bedroom].
189. Recommend sustainable living practices for reducing my environmental footprint, including [energy-saving tips, water conservation, or sustainable shopping habits].
190. Develop a plan for transitioning to a more minimalist lifestyle, focusing on [decluttering, simplifying daily routines, and reducing consumerism].
191. Suggest ways to reduce energy consumption in my home, including [using energy-efficient appliances, unplugging devices, or adjusting thermostat settings].
192. Create a plan for reducing plastic use in my daily life, including [switching to reusable bags, bottles, and containers].
193. Recommend sustainable shopping habits, including [buying second-hand, supporting ethical brands, or opting for eco-friendly packaging].
194. Provide strategies for reducing my carbon footprint when traveling, focusing on [public transportation, carpooling, or carbon offsets].

195. Develop a sustainable meal plan that focuses on reducing food waste, including [meal prepping, using leftovers, and composting].
196. Suggest ways to incorporate minimalism into my digital life, including [decluttering files, limiting screen time, and organizing digital spaces].
197. **Meta-Prompt:** Write a prompt that helps me design a plan to reduce my carbon footprint and live more sustainably, including [specific lifestyle changes like reducing waste, conserving energy, and supporting eco-friendly products].

Travel Planning

198. Create a 7-day itinerary for a trip to [specific destination, like Italy], including must-see attractions, local dining recommendations, and travel tips.
199. Suggest budget-friendly travel destinations for a [specific type of traveler, like solo traveler, family, or couple], focusing on [specific interests like adventure or relaxation].
200. Generate a packing list for a [specific type of trip, like beach vacation, business trip, or hiking adventure], including must-have essentials.
201. Provide recommendations for travel apps that help with [specific needs like language translation, booking accommodations, or finding restaurants].
202. Plan a weekend getaway to [specific nearby location], including activities, accommodations, and best times to visit.
203. Create a detailed road trip itinerary for [specific destination, like the Pacific Coast Highway], including scenic stops, hotels, and travel time estimates.
204. Suggest eco-friendly travel tips for reducing my carbon footprint while traveling to [specific destination or region].
205. Recommend travel safety tips for [specific country or region], including health precautions, transportation tips, and cultural norms.

206. Generate a list of local cuisine dishes to try when visiting [specific destination], with restaurant recommendations.
207. Provide advice on maximizing airline rewards or points for booking flights to [specific destination].
208. **Meta-Prompt:** Create a prompt that helps me plan a detailed itinerary for my next trip to [destination], ensuring it includes [accommodation, local attractions, and budget-friendly tips] while leaving room for relaxation and spontaneity.

Creative Writing and Journaling

209. Generate a daily journaling prompt for self-reflection, focusing on [specific areas like personal growth, gratitude, or productivity].
210. Create a writing prompt for a short story set in [specific location or time period], with the main character facing [specific challenge].
211. Suggest character development questions for a protagonist in a [specific genre, like mystery, fantasy, or romance] story.
212. Provide journaling prompts to explore [specific emotions like stress, joy, or motivation], helping me gain deeper insights.
213. Write the opening paragraph of a novel based on the theme of [specific theme, like overcoming adversity or discovering a secret].
214. Generate a poetry prompt that encourages the use of [specific literary device, like metaphors, similes, or alliteration], centered around [specific subject, like nature or love].
215. Create a list of creative journaling prompts to spark new ideas in areas like [specific interests, such as career, relationships, or hobbies].
216. Suggest writing prompts that focus on world-building for a [specific genre like sci-fi or fantasy] story, including key elements like geography, culture, and technology.

217. Generate a prompt to inspire reflective journaling about my goals for the next [specific time frame, like six months or one year].
218. Provide a list of writing prompts for exploring personal memories, focusing on [specific topics like childhood, major life events, or meaningful relationships].
219. **Meta-Prompt:** Develop a prompt that guides me in writing a short story or journal entry based on [specific theme or life experience], including ideas for character development, plot, and emotional depth.

Language Learning

220. Create a daily practice schedule for learning [specific language], including vocabulary drills, grammar exercises, and conversational practice.
221. Suggest language learning apps and tools for improving [specific language skill, like listening, speaking, or writing] in [specific language].
222. Generate a list of common phrases and vocabulary words for traveling to [specific country], focusing on [specific activities like ordering food, asking for directions, or shopping].
223. Provide language exercises to improve conversational skills in [specific language], using role-playing scenarios like [specific situations like job interviews, social events, or travel].
224. Write a short dialogue in [specific language] between two people discussing [specific topic, like work, family, or hobbies], and include a translation.
225. Suggest strategies for mastering the [specific language] alphabet and pronunciation, including helpful resources or tools.
226. Generate a daily language learning challenge for the next 30 days, focusing on improving [specific aspect like vocabulary or grammar] in [specific language].
227. Translate a paragraph from [specific language] to [another language], keeping the tone and context intact.

228. Recommend language immersion techniques for practicing [specific language] outside of formal lessons, such as [specific activities like watching movies, reading books, or speaking with native speakers].
229. Create a list of cultural tips for traveling to [specific country] to complement my [specific language] learning experience.
230. **Meta-Prompt:** Create a prompt that helps me develop a daily language learning plan, including [specific practice exercises for grammar, vocabulary, and conversation], ensuring that I stay motivated and track my progress.

Personal Branding

231. Provide tips for building a personal brand on [specific platform like LinkedIn], including profile optimization, content creation, and networking strategies.
232. Suggest strategies for improving my online presence as a [specific profession, like marketer, consultant, or entrepreneur], focusing on [specific area like showcasing expertise or increasing visibility].
233. Generate a list of content ideas for my [specific profession] blog that positions me as an authority in [specific industry or niche].
234. Write a compelling bio for my [specific platform like Instagram or Twitter] that highlights my skills, experience, and unique value proposition.
235. Recommend ways to improve my personal website to better reflect my brand identity and engage potential clients or employers.
236. Create a strategy for using social media to build relationships with [specific target audience, like potential clients or industry peers], including content types and posting frequency.
237. Suggest techniques for developing a strong personal narrative that can be used in [specific contexts like interviews, public speaking, or networking events].

238. Generate a list of achievements and projects to highlight on my portfolio to showcase my expertise in [specific field or industry].
239. Write a personal brand statement that captures my [specific strengths or expertise] and communicates my value to [specific target audience].
240. Provide strategies for growing my online influence through collaborations, guest posting, or [specific platforms like podcasts, webinars, or YouTube].
241. **Meta-Prompt:** Write a prompt that helps me craft a personal brand strategy for [specific social media platform like LinkedIn, Twitter, or Instagram], ensuring it highlights [my expertise, skills, and unique value proposition].

Work-Life Balance

242. Suggest strategies for maintaining a healthy work-life balance while working from home, including boundaries, time management, and self-care.
243. Generate a weekly schedule that prioritizes work tasks, family time, and self-care activities, ensuring balance across all areas.
244. Recommend tips for managing stress and avoiding burnout while juggling [specific commitments like work, family, and personal projects].
245. Create a daily routine that includes high-priority work time, breaks, and activities to recharge, helping me maintain productivity without overworking.
246. Provide suggestions for creating boundaries between work and personal life, including strategies for [specific scenarios like turning off notifications or setting designated work hours].
247. Generate a list of self-care practices I can incorporate into my daily routine to improve my mental, emotional, and physical well-being.
248. Recommend time management techniques to help me stay on top of work tasks while still making time for hobbies and personal growth.

249. Provide a list of stress-relief activities I can engage in during the workday to reset and stay focused.
250. Suggest ways to disconnect and unwind after a long workday, ensuring I fully recharge for the next day.
251. Create a weekend routine that focuses on rest, relaxation, and personal development, helping me recover from a busy week.
252. **Meta-Prompt:** Create a prompt that helps me build a daily routine that promotes work-life balance, incorporating [work hours, family time, and self-care activities], ensuring that I maintain both productivity and personal well-being.

Home Décor and Design

253. Suggest color schemes for a [specific room like living room, bedroom, or kitchen], focusing on [specific styles like modern, cozy, or minimalist].
254. Generate ideas for rearranging furniture in my [specific room] to create a more functional and aesthetically pleasing layout.
255. Provide tips for decorating a [specific room or space] on a budget, including DIY projects and affordable design elements.
256. Recommend design ideas for making a small space feel larger, using strategies like [specific techniques such as lighting, mirrors, or multipurpose furniture].
257. Create a plan for updating the décor in my [specific room], incorporating trends like [farmhouse chic, industrial, boho, etc.].
258. Suggest ways to incorporate eco-friendly design elements into my home, focusing on [specific materials like reclaimed wood, bamboo, or energy-efficient lighting].
259. Generate DIY project ideas for creating custom home décor, using materials like [wood, fabric, or metal].
260. Provide ideas for creating a cozy reading nook or workspace in my [specific room, such as living room or bedroom], including furniture and lighting suggestions.

261. Recommend design tips for improving the curb appeal of my home, including suggestions for [specific improvements like landscaping, paint colors, or lighting].
262. Suggest ways to personalize my home décor using family photos, keepsakes, or custom art, focusing on creating a unique and meaningful space.
263. **Meta-Prompt:** Generate a prompt that helps me design a room makeover plan, including [color schemes, furniture layouts, and DIY décor ideas] based on the style and functionality I want to achieve.

Party Planning

264. Suggest creative party themes for a [specific occasion like a birthday, anniversary, or holiday], including decorations, games, and food ideas.
265. Generate a shopping list for a [specific number of guests] dinner party, including ingredients for a [specific menu type, like a three-course meal, BBQ, or brunch].
266. Recommend activities and games for a [specific type of party like a family gathering, office party, or kids' birthday], ensuring everyone is engaged and entertained.
267. Create a timeline for organizing a party, including critical milestones like sending invitations, decorating, and preparing food.
268. Provide ideas for hosting a virtual party, including games, activities, and ways to keep guests engaged online.
269. Suggest a menu for a [specific type of event like potluck, picnic, or cocktail party], focusing on easy-to-make and crowd-pleasing dishes.
270. Generate a list of creative DIY decoration ideas for a themed party, using affordable materials like [specific materials, such as paper, fabric, or balloons].
271. Recommend ways to incorporate a theme into a party through [specific elements like food, music, and décor], ensuring everything feels cohesive.

272. Suggest icebreaker questions or conversation starters for guests at a party, focusing on creating fun and engaging discussions.
273. Provide a checklist of essentials for hosting a successful party, including [specific categories like food, drinks, music, and seating arrangements].
274. **Meta-Prompt:** Develop a prompt that helps me organize a party, including [the theme, guest list, menu, and activity ideas], ensuring it's a memorable event with personalized touches.

Crafting and DIY Projects

275. Generate ideas for DIY craft projects using recycled materials like [specific materials such as cardboard, glass jars, or fabric scraps].
276. Provide step-by-step instructions for creating homemade gifts like [specific items, such as candles, photo frames, or knitted scarves].
277. Suggest easy craft projects for beginners using common household materials, like [specific materials such as paper, glue, and string].
278. Recommend DIY holiday decorations for [specific holidays, like Christmas, Halloween, or Thanksgiving], focusing on affordable and creative ideas.
279. Create a list of DIY home improvement projects for beginners, including [specific projects like painting a room, installing shelves, or updating light fixtures].
280. Suggest craft ideas for kids using materials like [markers, construction paper, clay, etc.], ensuring the activities are fun and educational.
281. Provide instructions for creating personalized home décor items like [specific items like wall art, pillows, or planters], adding a custom touch to my space.

282. Recommend craft ideas for [specific events like weddings, baby showers, or birthdays], focusing on creating meaningful and memorable decorations or favors.
283. Generate ideas for upcycling old furniture or clothing into new, functional items, using [specific techniques like painting, sewing, or refinishing].
284. Suggest DIY projects for organizing my home, such as creating [specific items like storage bins, drawer dividers, or shelving units].
285. **Meta-Prompt:** Create a prompt that helps me come up with creative DIY craft ideas based on [available materials or themes like holidays, personal gifts, or home décor], ensuring they are fun and easy to execute.

Games and Entertainment

286. Create trivia questions on the topic of [specific subject like movies, history, or science], including multiple-choice answers.
287. Generate a list of fun party games for [specific number of people], focusing on [specific types of games, like icebreakers, board games, or outdoor activities].
288. Suggest ideas for a themed game night, including [specific themes like 80s trivia, murder mystery, or board game tournament].
289. Write out instructions for creating a DIY scavenger hunt, including clues and locations for a [specific type of event like a birthday party or family gathering].
290. Provide ideas for virtual games that can be played over video calls, such as [specific games like trivia, charades, or Pictionary].
291. Suggest creative quiz ideas for a [specific audience, like friends, family, or coworkers], focusing on [specific topics like pop culture, travel, or personal trivia].
292. Generate questions for a "Would You Rather" game tailored to [specific themes like work, relationships, or travel].

293. Create a list of classic card games or board games that are suitable for [specific age group, like kids, teens, or adults].
294. Recommend cooperative games for groups, focusing on [specific genres like strategy, adventure, or problem-solving games].
295. Write out the rules for a DIY version of [specific game, like Bingo or Jeopardy], including materials needed and gameplay instructions.
296. **Meta-Prompt:** Write a prompt that helps me create trivia questions or interactive quizzes for [specific event like game night or a party], ensuring they are engaging and fun for all participants.

Discovering New Tools

297. Recommend AI tools for improving productivity and task management, focusing on [specific needs like project tracking, communication, or automation].
298. Suggest new apps for organizing personal finances, including tools for budgeting, tracking expenses, and managing investments.
299. Provide a list of tools for improving creative workflows, focusing on [specific areas like design, writing, or video editing].
300. Recommend AI-powered research tools for gathering data and insights in [specific field, like marketing, health, or education].
301. Suggest apps for improving time management, focusing on [specific features like time-blocking, setting reminders, and tracking progress].
302. Provide a list of tools for streamlining remote work, including apps for [specific tasks like team communication, document sharing, or project collaboration].
303. Recommend apps for improving mental well-being, including tools for [specific needs like meditation, stress management, or sleep tracking].

304. Suggest tools for automating social media content creation and scheduling, focusing on [specific platforms like Instagram, Twitter, or LinkedIn].
305. Provide a list of tools for organizing digital clutter, such as apps for managing [specific types of files like photos, emails, or documents].
306. Recommend tools for learning new skills, including apps for [specific areas like coding, languages, or creative arts].
307. **Meta-Prompt:** Generate a prompt that suggests the latest and most relevant AI tools or productivity apps for [specific tasks like project management, design, or personal finance], ensuring they improve workflow and efficiency.

Workplace Communication and Collaboration

308. Draft an email to [team member's name] requesting feedback on our current project, highlighting specific areas where their input would be most valuable.
309. Generate talking points for an upcoming team meeting, focusing on project updates and ways to improve collaboration.
310. Create a step-by-step guide for resolving a disagreement with a colleague in a professional and constructive manner.
311. Suggest strategies for improving communication within a remote team, ensuring clear task delegation and accountability.
312. Draft an email to [team member's name] recognizing their contributions and providing constructive feedback on areas for improvement.
313. Create a weekly check-in structure for remote teams to keep communication smooth and progress visible.
314. Generate a list of questions to ask during a one-on-one meeting with my supervisor to get feedback on my performance.

315. Recommend strategies to enhance collaboration between departments involved in the same project, ensuring alignment of goals and objectives.
316. Create an agenda for a team brainstorming session focused on [specific project or problem] and outline roles for each participant.
317. Generate suggestions for virtual team-building activities to improve morale and communication in a remote environment.
318. **Meta-Prompt:** Create a prompt that helps me run more effective team meetings, including suggestions for [setting agendas, encouraging individual participation, and following up on action items].

Mindset and Motivation

319. Create a daily affirmation routine that helps boost my confidence and motivation before starting work.
320. Suggest ways to overcome procrastination when working on long-term projects with distant deadlines.
321. Generate a list of morning habits that will help me start the day with a positive mindset and focused energy.
322. Write a daily journal prompt that encourages self-reflection on how I can stay motivated to achieve my personal and professional goals.
323. Suggest strategies for maintaining a positive mindset when facing setbacks or unexpected challenges in my work.
324. Create a weekly motivation plan, including reminders, for staying focused on long-term goals despite short-term distractions.
325. Generate a set of mental exercises to build resilience and stay motivated during high-pressure situations.
326. Provide a list of practical tips for avoiding burnout and maintaining enthusiasm for [specific project or work task].
327. Suggest ways to celebrate small wins to maintain momentum and motivation throughout the week.

328. Develop a reward system that incentivizes me to complete daily and weekly tasks with consistent effort and focus.
329. **Meta-Prompt:** Develop a prompt that guides me in setting a weekly intention that aligns with my personal and professional goals, ensuring it includes actions for staying accountable and reflecting on progress.

Creativity and Innovation

330. Generate three innovative solutions for [specific business challenge or creative project] that I'm currently facing.
331. Suggest creative brainstorming techniques that can help me come up with unique ideas for [specific task or project].
332. Create a step-by-step guide for overcoming creative blocks when working on [specific type of work or project].
333. Develop a weekly schedule that includes dedicated time for brainstorming and creative thinking every day.
334. Generate a list of creative ways to engage customers or clients with a new product or service launch.
335. Suggest exercises that can stimulate creativity when I feel stuck in the middle of a project.
336. Generate prompts for a team brainstorming session that will inspire out-of-the-box ideas for [specific project].
337. Suggest tools or apps that can enhance creativity and innovation in daily work tasks.
338. Write a reflective journaling prompt to help me assess and improve my creative process.
339. Recommend new methods for experimenting with innovative ideas in [specific area of work], helping me push boundaries and think differently.
340. **Meta-Prompt:** Generate a prompt that helps me brainstorm innovative solutions for [a specific business challenge or creative project], encouraging out-of-the-box thinking and new approaches to solving the problem.

Creating ChatGPT Effective Prompts

341. **Meta-Prompt:** Write a prompt that helps me create more effective ChatGPT prompts. It should focus on structuring clear instructions, providing sufficient context, and specifying desired outcomes to achieve accurate and actionable responses from ChatGPT.
342. **Meta-Prompt:** Write a prompt that helps me create clear and goal-oriented ChatGPT prompts. It should guide me on how to explicitly define the end result I'm looking for, ensuring ChatGPT understands the objective and provides relevant, actionable responses.
343. **Meta-Prompt:** Help me craft a prompt that encourages detailed responses from ChatGPT. It should show me how to ask specific questions, include necessary context, and outline all relevant variables to get the most accurate and helpful results.
344. **Meta-Prompt:** Write a prompt that helps me tailor ChatGPT prompts for tone and style. It should teach me how to specify the desired tone (formal, casual, motivational) or writing style (informative, creative, conversational) for better alignment with my needs.
345. **Meta-Prompt:** Create a prompt that guides me in refining and iterating ChatGPT prompts. It should instruct me on how to evaluate initial results, tweak the input, and reframe questions to improve the output until I get the desired response.
346. **Meta-Prompt:** Help me craft a prompt that teaches me how to include examples when asking ChatGPT for complex or specific tasks. It should show me how to provide sample data or scenarios to clarify what I want in the response.
347. **Meta-Prompt:** Write a prompt that guides me on creating effective ChatGPT prompts when the task or question is broad or ambiguous. It should instruct me on how to ask for clarification or specify what assumptions ChatGPT should make to avoid misunderstandings.

348. **Meta-Prompt:** Help me develop a prompt that ensures I give ChatGPT enough context for nuanced responses. It should teach me how to provide background information, relevant details, and any necessary constraints to improve the accuracy of ChatGPT's output.
349. **Meta-Prompt:** Create a prompt that helps me design ChatGPT prompts to generate actionable suggestions. It should show me how to ask for step-by-step guidance or solutions, ensuring the response is practical and can be easily implemented.
350. **Meta-Prompt:** Write a prompt that guides me on how to balance between asking ChatGPT broad, exploratory questions and specific, narrow tasks. It should teach me when to use open-ended questions versus targeted instructions for different types of queries.

CONCLUSION

You've made it to the end of *AI Mastery for Beginners: Simple Strategies and Exercises to Boost Productivity, Spark Creativity, and Advance Your Career*! Now is an excellent time to reflect on what you knew before reading this book. Maybe AI felt unfamiliar or overwhelming. Perhaps you didn't realize how much AI you were already using. Or maybe you knew you wanted to broaden your understanding but weren't sure where to begin. At this point, you've navigated the complexities of AI, mastered essential tools, and built a solid foundation for easily integrating AI into your lifestyle. This progress sets you ahead of the curve, ready to approach the future with confidence.

Where do you go from here? How will you tap into the power of AI to transform your daily routine and enrich your life? Maybe you'll start a project where AI helps streamline your work or dive deeper into tools that help you achieve personal goals, such as mastering a new skill or exploring a creative passion. Apply what you've learned—don't be afraid to experiment or get a little messy. Revisit the hands-on exercises, refine your approach, and watch how quickly your skills evolve.

Learning doesn't stop here. AI is an ever-evolving field, which is exactly what makes it so exciting—there's always more to discover, experiment with, and push the boundaries of. As new developments emerge, you'll already be equipped with a solid understanding of the fundamentals, giving you the flexibility to adapt and grow.

While continuing on this path, remember that AI is not just a tool; it's your ally—a resource to help solve problems, boost productivity, and unlock new opportunities. Whether you're looking to elevate your career, simplify your personal life, or expand your creative pursuits, AI is there to support your vision. This journey is ongoing, and the most exciting part is that you're in control. With AI as your partner, you have the power to shape your future. No matter where you go next, the knowledge and skills you've gained will continue empowering you to reach new heights. YOU are the architect of your AI-powered future.

So, here's to your continued success and the endless possibilities ahead. Stay curious, keep learning, and let AI propel you toward a more productive, creative, and fulfilling life. The future is in your hands, and I can't wait to see what you achieve!

YOUR WORDS KEEP THE JOURNEY GOING

If this book supported your journey and you feel it earned a 5-star review, I'd be so grateful if you'd take a moment to share your thoughts.

Your words could be exactly what someone else needs to feel confident starting their own AI journey. Most people rely on reviews to decide if a book is worth their time, and *your perspective matters*.

Leaving a review is **quick**, **free**, and makes a real impact by helping more people discover how AI can simplify their lives, spark creativity, and unlock new opportunities.

Ready to make a difference? Scan the QR code below to leave your review.

Thank you for helping others take their first step into the world of AI!

Yours in curiosity and growth,
Maura Vella

GLOSSARY

Acorns: An investment app that rounds up your spare change from purchases and invests it in a diversified portfolio. https://www.acorns.com/

AI (Artificial Intelligence): A field of computer science focused on creating systems that can perform tasks that typically require human intelligence, such as learning, problem-solving, and decision-making.

AIGardenPlanner : An AI-powered application that provides personalized garden designs and planting plans based on user preferences and garden conditions. https://aigardenplanner.com/

Alexa: Amazon's virtual assistant that performs tasks like playing music, providing weather updates, and controlling smart home devices. https://www.alexa.com/

Algorithm: A series of instructions or rules followed by a computer to perform a task or solve a problem. In AI, algorithms process data to learn patterns and make decisions.

Algorithmic Bias: The tendency of an AI algorithm to produce unfair or prejudiced outcomes, often as a result of the data it was trained on, which can lead to discrimination against certain groups.

Algorithm Transparency: The principle that AI algorithms should be understandable and interpretable allowing users to know how decisions are being made, particularly in areas like finance, healthcare, and criminal justice where transparency is crucial.

Amazon: A global e-commerce platform that utilizes AI to power services like product recommendations and voice-activated virtual assistants like Alexa. https://www.amazon.com/

Amazon Echo: A smart speaker equipped with Alexa, designed to control smart home devices, play music, and provide information. My Book

Anonymization: The process where personal data is stripped of identifying information, making it impossible to trace back to an individual.

Apple Calendar: A scheduling app for Apple devices that syncs events, sets reminders, and integrates with other apps for efficient time management. https://apps.apple.com/us/app/calendar/id1108185179

Apple Health: A health and fitness tracking app that consolidates health data from various sources into a single dashboard on iOS devices. https://www.apple.com/health/

Apple Reminders: A task management app for Apple devices that organizes tasks and sends notifications. https://apps.apple.com/us/app/reminders/id1108187841

Apple Watch: A wearable device by Apple that tracks fitness, health, and lifestyle metrics. https://www.apple.com/watch/

Applicant Tracking Systems (ATS): Software that automates the hiring process by filtering resumes and ranking candidates.

Artbreeder: An AI-powered platform that allows users to create and modify images, combining different features to generate unique art. https://www.artbreeder.com/

Augmented Reality (AR): Technology that overlays digital content on the real world through devices like smartphones or AR glasses.

August Smart Lock: A smart lock for homes that can be controlled remotely or integrated with voice assistants. https://august.com/

Bias: Systematic errors in AI models or data that lead to unfair or inaccurate outcomes.

Buffer: A social media management platform that uses AI to schedule and optimize posts across various platforms. https://buffer.com/

Calendly: A scheduling tool that helps automate meeting bookings, integrating with calendars to streamline availability. https://calendly.com/

Calm: An app for guided meditation, sleep stories, and stress relief exercises. https://www.calm.com/

Canva: An online design platform that uses AI to help users create graphics, presentations, and social media content. https://www.canva.com/

Chatbot: An AI-powered program that simulates human conversation, commonly used for customer service, answering questions, and automating tasks.

ChatGPT: A conversational AI developed by OpenAI that generates human-like text in response to prompts. https://chatgpt.com/

Content Marketing: A strategy that uses AI to create and optimize content for engaging a target audience.

Copy.ai: A platform for generating marketing copy, blog posts, and other written content with AI assistance. http://Copy.ai

DALL-E: An AI system by OpenAI that generates images from text descriptions. https://openai.com/index/dall-e-3/

Data: Information processed by AI to identify patterns, make decisions, and generate insights.

Data Bias: When datasets used to train AI systems are skewed or unrepresentative, leading to biased outcomes in AI decisions.

Dataset: A collection of data used to train AI models; its quality impacts model performance.

Data Minimization: A privacy principle where only the necessary data is collected and used for its intended purpose.

Data Privacy: Practices that ensure personal data is protected and only used for authorized purposes.

Deep Learning: A subset of machine learning involving neural networks with many layers, allowing AI systems to learn complex patterns in large datasets.

Diverse and Representative Datasets: Datasets that include a wide range of demographic and contextual data, reducing bias in AI models and improving accuracy.

Duolingo: A language-learning app that uses AI to adapt lessons to users' proficiency and progress, making learning interactive and fun. https://www.duolingo.com/

Edge AI: AI that processes data locally on devices instead of relying on cloud servers.

Empower: A financial platform that offers tools to manage investments, track finances, and plan for retirement. https://www.empower.com/

Ethical AI: The practice of designing AI systems that prioritize fairness, transparency, and respect for user rights.

Explainable AI (XAI): AI systems that provide clear, understandable explanations for their decisions, making them more transparent and trustworthy.

Exploding Topics: A tool that identifies emerging trends with AI, helping businesses stay competitive. https://explodingtopics.com/

Facial Recognition Technology: AI-based software that identifies individuals by analyzing facial features, often used for security.

Fitbit: A fitness tracker monitoring physical activity, sleep, and health metrics, offering insights powered by AI.

Fitbod: A workout planning app that uses AI to create personalized strength training routines based on your progress. https://fitbod.me/

Generative AI: A type of AI that creates new content, such as text, images, music, video generation, or 3D model creation by learning patterns from existing data.

Google: A search engine and technology company that utilizes AI in various products, from search algorithms to Google Assistant. https://www.google.com/

Google Assistant: A voice-activated AI assistant that integrates with smart devices and performs various tasks. https://assistant.google.com/

Google Calendar: A scheduling tool that integrates with AI to manage events, send reminders, and sync across devices for seamless time management. https://calendar.google.com/

Google Fit: A health platform that tracks physical activity and health data across devices. https://www.google.com/fit/

Google Home: A smart home platform that integrates with Google Assistant, enabling voice control and automation of connected devices such as lights, thermostats, and speakers. https://home.google.com/

Google Maps: A mapping service enhanced by AI for real-time traffic updates and route optimization. https://www.google.com/maps

Google Photos: A cloud-based photo storage and management service that uses AI for photo organization, search, and editing. https://www.google.com/photos/

Google Shopping: An AI-powered platform that allows users to compare products and prices across various online retailers. https://shopping.google.com/

Google Tasks: A simple task management app that helps users create, organize, and track to-do lists across devices. https://tasks.google.com/

Google Travel: A platform for managing bookings, itineraries, and travel recommendations, with features like price tracking and personalized suggestions. https://www.google.com/travel/

Grammarly: A writing assistant that uses AI to enhance grammar, clarity, and style. https://www.grammarly.com/

Headspace: A meditation app with tools for mindfulness, relaxation, and stress management. https://www.headspace.com/

Honey: An AI-powered browser extension that finds and applies the best discount codes at checkout and tracks price trends to save you money. https://www.joinhoney.com/

Hootsuite: A social media management platform that uses AI to help users schedule, track, and optimize social media posts. https://www.hootsuite.com

Informed Consent: A process ensuring individuals receive clear information about the risks and benefits of sharing personal data.

IdeaBuddy: A business planning tool that uses AI to help brainstorm, develop, and validate ideas. https://ideabuddy.com/

Jasper.ai: An AI tool for creating content like blog posts, marketing copy, and other written materials. http://Jasper.ai

Jobscan: A platform that increases resume visibility by using AI to optimize them for Applicant Tracking Systems (ATS). https://www.jobscan.co/

JRNY: A fitness app that tailors workout plans based on individual goals and progress using AI. https://www.jrny.com/

Kayak: A travel search engine that uses AI to compare flights, hotels, and car rentals, providing users with the best deals. https://www.kayak.com/

Landbot: A no-code chatbot platform that automates customer interactions and feedback through engaging, customizable conversations. https://landbot.io/

Lately.ai: An AI-powered social media marketing tool that repurposes content and generates social posts based on user input. http://Lately.ai

Lifesum: A health app that tracks nutrition, exercise, and well-being, offering AI-driven recommendations for healthy living. https://lifesum.com/

LIFX: Smart light bulbs that integrate with voice assistants to automate lighting and create ambiance. https://www.lifx.com/

Luminar Neo: AI photo editing software that simplifies complex tasks, enhances creativity, and delivers professional-quality results. https://skylum.com/luminar

Manychat: A chatbot platform enabling businesses to create automated messaging experiences for customer engagement. https://manychat.com/

MasterClass: An online platform offering video-based courses taught by experts in various fields. https://www.masterclass.com/

Meta-Prompt: A prompt that instructs AI to design a customized prompt based on specific goals or preferences.

Microsoft Co-Pilot: An AI assistant in Microsoft 365 that simplifies tasks like document creation and data analysis. https://copilot.microsoft.com/

MidJourney: A creative tool that generates high-quality images from text descriptions using AI. https://www.midjourney.com/

Muse: A wearable device that uses AI to monitor brain activity and provide real-time feedback during meditation, helping users improve focus, relaxation, and mindfulness. https://choosemuse.com/

MyFitnessPal: A nutrition and fitness tracker that helps users achieve goals through calorie tracking and AI-powered insights. https://www.myfitnesspal.com/

Neural Networks: Machine learning models inspired by the human brain, enabling AI to recognize patterns and make decisions.

Noom: A health app focused on behavior change, using AI to provide coaching for weight loss and fitness. https://www.noom.com/

OpenAI: An organization pioneering AI advancements, including GPT and DALL-E.

Organizing Data: Structuring information so AI systems can analyze it effectively and generate insights.

Oura: A smart ring that monitors health metrics and provides personalized insights through AI analysis. https://ouraring.com/

Outlook: A scheduling and email tool that manages events, reminders, and tasks while syncing across devices for streamlined productivity. https://www.microsoft.com/en-us/microsoft-365/outlook/

Peloton Guide: A fitness device that combines classes with AI-powered performance tracking and feedback. https://www.onepeloton.com/guide

Philips Hue: A smart lighting system controllable via apps or AI assistants like Alexa and Google Assistant. https://www.philips-hue.com/

Plantix: A gardening app that uses AI to diagnose crop issues through photo analysis and provides treatment suggestions to improve plant health. https://plantix.net/en/

PocketGuard: A budgeting app that simplifies financial tracking by calculating disposable income and monitoring expenses https://pocketguard.com/

Proactive Engagement: AI's ability to anticipate user needs and respond without being prompted, enhancing experiences.

Procreate: A digital art app designed for tablets, featuring AI-assisted tools like predictive brushstrokes and layering options for professional-quality creations. https://procreate.com/

Prompt: The input or instruction provided to an AI system to generate a response or complete a task.

QuillBot: A writing tool that uses AI to paraphrase, improve clarity, and optimize grammar. https://quillbot.com/

Reclaim.ai: A scheduling app that prioritizes and arranges tasks around meetings with AI automation. http://Reclaim.ai

Reddit: A platform that recommends relevant posts to users based on their interests and behaviors using AI. https://www.reddit.com/

Resume.io: A resume builder that uses AI to create tailored, optimized resumes for specific job applications. http://Resume.io

Ring: A smart security device that uses AI-powered cameras to monitor and protect homes in real time. https://ring.com/

Rufus: Amazon's AI-powered shopping assistant that provides real-time product recommendations and answers based on your preferences and browsing habits.

Runway ML: A creative platform that generates videos, images, and animations from text prompts using AI. https://runwayml.com/

Segments (Customer): Groups of users categorized by AI tools based on behaviors or preferences, enabling targeted marketing.

Sentiment Analysis: AI technology that detects and classifies emotions in text, often used for customer feedback analysis.

SEO (Search Engine Optimization): Optimizing websites to improve search engine visibility and drive organic traffic.

ShopSavvy: An app that compares product prices across retailers using AI to find the best deals. https://shopsavvy.com/

Shortcuts: An Apple automation tool that streamlines tasks by creating custom routines. https://apps.apple.com/us/app/shortcuts/id915249334

SideChef: A cooking app offering recipe recommendations and guided instructions tailored to user preferences with AI. https://www.sidechef.com/

Siri: Apple's virtual assistant for managing tasks like reminders, messages, and smart home controls. https://www.apple.com/siri/

Skillshare: An online platform offering courses on topics from design to business skills. https://www.skillshare.com/

Skyscanner: A travel app that uses AI to identify the best deals on flights, hotels, and car rentals. https://www.skyscanner.com/

Smart Home Devices: Devices that automate tasks like lighting, heating, and security using AI technology.

Societal Bias: AI systems reflecting biases present in the society that created them, often perpetuating inequities.

Spotify: A music streaming service that uses AI to recommend personalized playlists and content. https://www.spotify.com/

Strava: A fitness app tracking activity with AI-driven performance analysis and insights. https://www.strava.com/

Tempo Studio: A comprehensive home fitness system that uses AI technology to provide a personalized workout experience. https://tempo.fit/

The Foundational Principles of Ethical AI: Core principles like fairness, transparency, and accountability guiding responsible AI use.

TripIt: A travel management app that organizes bookings and itineraries with AI-driven insights. https://www.tripit.com/web

Two-Factor Authentication: A security measure requiring two verification methods for accessing sensitive data.

Viome: An AI-driven platform that analyzes gut microbiome data to provide personalized dietary and supplement recommendations. https://www.viome.com/

Virtual Assistant: AI software that performs tasks like scheduling, reminders, and answering queries through voice or text.

Virtual Reality (VR): Immersive technology creating digital environments, often enhanced by AI for realistic simulations.

Voice Assistants: AI systems like Alexa and Google Assistant that respond to voice commands to perform tasks.

Whoop Strap: A fitness tracker that uses AI to monitor metrics like sleep, recovery, and activity. https://www.whoop.com/

YNAB: A budgeting app that tracks spending and helps plan finances using AI. https://www.ynab.com/

Yousician: A music learning app offering lessons and feedback for instruments through AI analysis. https://yousician.com/

YouTube: A video platform that uses AI algorithms to recommend videos based on user preferences. https://www.youtube.com/

Zoom: A video conferencing app enhanced by AI for noise suppression and optimized video quality. https://zoom.us/

REFERENCES

Acorns. (n.d.). Retrieved from https://www.acorns.com/

AIGardenPlanner. (n.d.). Retrieved from https://aigardenplanner.com/

AI Scheduling Assistant: Top 10 Tools for 2024 (Tested). (n.d.). Retrieved from https://www.meetjamie.ai/blog/ai-scheduling-assistant

Alexa. (n.d.). Amazon. Retrieved from https://www.amazon.com/

Amazon. (2024, September 19). Amazon's gen AI personalizes product recommendations and descriptions. Retrieved from https://www.aboutamazon.com/news/retail/amazon-generative-ai-product-search-results-and-descriptions

Amazon Echo. (n.d.). Amazon. Retrieved from https://www.amazon.com/

Apple Health. (n.d.). Apple. Retrieved from https://www.apple.com/

Apple Watch. (n.d.). Apple. Retrieved from https://www.apple.com/

Artbreeder. (n.d.). Retrieved from https://www.artbreeder.com/

Atreya, S. (2023). Data Quality For Good AI Outcomes. *Forbes*. Retrieved from https://www.forbes.com/sites/garydrenik/2023/08/15/data-quality-for-good-ai-outcomes/

August Smart Lock. (n.d.). Retrieved from https://august.com/

Bloomreach. (2024, August 21). The Rise of AI-Powered Personal Shopping Services. Retrieved from https://www.bloomreach.com/en/blog/ai-powered-personal-shopping-services

Buffer. (n.d.). Retrieved from https://buffer.com/

Calendly. (n.d.). Retrieved from https://calendly.com/

Calm. (n.d.). Retrieved from https://www.calm.com/

Canva. (n.d.). Retrieved from https://www.canva.com/

ChatBot.com. (n.d.). Benefits of AI in customer service. Retrieved from https://www.chatbot.com/blog/benefits-of-ai-in-customer-service/

ChatGPT. (n.d.). OpenAI. Retrieved from https://www.openai.com/

CNET. (2023, June 15). Can an AI-powered fitness app outperform a human trainer? Retrieved from https://www.cnet.com/tech/can-an-ai-powered-fitness-app-outperform-a-human-trainer/

Copy.ai. (n.d.). Retrieved from https://www.copy.ai/

DALL-E. (n.d.). OpenAI. Retrieved from https://www.openai.com/

De Gasperis, T. (2020). *Futures of Responsible and Inclusive AI: How Might We Foster an Inclusive, Responsible and Foresight-Informed AI Governance Approach?* Retrieved from https://core.ac.uk/download/376476397.pdf

DevRev. (2024). 11 examples of AI customer service to consider in 2024. Retrieved from https://devrev.com/blog/examples-of-ai-customer-service/

Duolingo. (n.d.). Retrieved from https://www.duolingo.com/

Empower. (n.d.). Retrieved from https://www.empower.com

Exploding Topics. (n.d.). Retrieved from https://explodingtopics.com

Fitbit. (n.d.). Retrieved from https://www.fitbit.com/

Fitbod. (n.d.). Retrieved from https://fitbod.me/

Google Assistant. (n.d.). Google. Retrieved from https://assistant.google.com/

Google Fit. (n.d.). Google. Retrieved from https://fit.google.com/

Google Maps. (n.d.). Google. Retrieved from https://maps.google.com/

Google Photos. (n.d.). Google. Retrieved from https://photos.google.com/

Google Shopping. (n.d.). Google. Retrieved from https://shopping.google.com/

Google Travel. (n.d.). Google. Retrieved from https://www.google.com/travel/

Grammarly. (n.d.). Retrieved from https://www.grammarly.com/

Headspace. (n.d.). Retrieved from https://www.headspace.com/

Helal, S., & Bull, C. N. (2020). From smart homes to smart-ready homes and communities. *IEEE Pervasive Computing, 19*(2), 69-73. https://doi.org/10.1109/mprv.2020.2977739

Honey. (n.d.). Retrieved from https://www.joinhoney.com/

Hootsuite. (n.d.). Retrieved from https://www.hootsuite.com/

Human Made. (2024). AI ethics in focus: Addressing bias, privacy, and transparency challenges. Retrieved from https://humanmade.com/ai/ethics-in-ai/

IdeaBuddy. (n.d.). Retrieved from https://www.ideabuddy.com/

IBM. (n.d.). What is edge AI? Retrieved from https://www.ibm.com/topics/edge-ai

Jasper.ai. (n.d.). Retrieved from https://www.jasper.ai/

Jobscan. (n.d.). Retrieved from https://www.jobscan.co/

JRNY. (n.d.). Retrieved from https://www.bowflex.com/jrny.html

Kayak. (n.d.). Retrieved from https://www.kayak.com/

Landbot. (n.d.). Retrieved from https://landbot.io

Lately.ai. (n.d.). Retrieved from https://www.lately.ai/

Lifesum. (n.d.). Retrieved from https://www.lifesum.com/

LIFX. (n.d.). Retrieved from https://www.lifx.com/

Maryville University. (n.d.). History of AI: Timeline and the Future. Retrieved from https://online.maryville.edu/blog/history-of-ai/

MasterClass. (n.d.). Retrieved from https://www.masterclass.com/

Microsoft. (n.d.). *Introducing Microsoft 365 Copilot: Your copilot for work*. Retrieved from https://www.microsoft.com/en-us/microsoft-365/copilot

MidJourney. (n.d.). Retrieved from https://www.midjourney.com/

Muse. (n.d.). Retrieved from https://choosemuse.com

MyFitnessPal. (n.d.). Retrieved from https://www.myfitnesspal.com/

Noom. (n.d.). Retrieved from https://www.noom.com/

OpenAI. (2024). ChatGPT (October 18 version) [Large language model]. Retrieved from https://chat.openai.com/

Oura. (n.d.). Retrieved from https://ouraring.com/

Peloton Guide. (n.d.). Retrieved from https://www.onepeloton.com/

Philips Hue. (n.d.). Philips. Retrieved from https://www.philips-hue.com/

Plantix. (n.d.). Retrieved from https://plantix.net/en/

Procreate. (n.d.). Retrieved from https://procreate.art/

QuillBot. (n.d.). Retrieved from https://quillbot.com/

Reclaim.ai. (n.d.). Retrieved from https://reclaim.ai/

Resume.io. (n.d.). Retrieved from https://resume.io/

Ring. (n.d.). Amazon. Retrieved from https://ring.com/

Runway ML. (n.d.). Retrieved from https://runwayml.com/

ShopSavvy. (n.d.). Retrieved from https://shopsavvy.com/
SideChef. (n.d.). Retrieved from https://www.sidechef.com/
Siri. (n.d.). Apple. Retrieved from https://www.apple.com/siri/
Skillshare. (n.d.). Retrieved from https://www.skillshare.com/
Skylum. (n.d.). Retrieved from https://skylum.com/luminar
Skyscanner. (n.d.). Retrieved from https://www.skyscanner.com/
Spotify. (n.d.). Retrieved from https://www.spotify.com/
Strava. (n.d.). Retrieved from https://www.strava.com/
Tempo Studio. (n.d.). Retrieved from https://tempo.fit/
TripIt. (n.d.). Retrieved from https://www.tripit.com/
Viome. (n.d.). Retrieved from https://www.viome.com/
Virtasant. (2024). AI-driven customer engagement: Strategies from Amazon, Nike, and Hilton. Retrieved from https://www.virtasant.com/ai-today/ai-driven-customer-engagement-strategies-from-amazon-nike-and-hilton
YNAB (You Need A Budget). (n.d.). Retrieved from https://www.ynab.com/
YouTube. (n.d.). Google. Retrieved from https://www.youtube.com/
Yousician. (n.d.). Retrieved from https://yousician.com/
Zoom. (n.d.). Retrieved from https://zoom.us/

www.ingramcontent.com/pod-product-compliance
Lightning Source LLC
LaVergne TN
LVHW022220200926
848481LV00006B/2040
* 9 7 9 8 3 4 8 5 9 3 1 7 9 *